IRON BRITANNIA

IRON BRITANNIA

Anthony Barnett

Allison and Busby
London

First published 1982 by
Allison & Busby Ltd
6a Noel Street
London W1V 3RB

British Library Cataloguing in Publication Data

Barnett, Anthony
  Iron Britannia.
  1. Falkland Islands War, 1982
  2. Falkland Islands—Politics and government
  I. Title
  997'.11   F3031

  ISBN 0-85031-494-1
  ISBN 0-85031-493-3 Pbk

Set in 10/11 Baskerville by
Derek Doyle & Associates, Mold, Clwyd.
Printed in Great Britain by
Richard Clay (The Chaucer Press) Ltd, Bungay, Suffolk.

Contents

Judith

Preface and Thanks

This essay was begun on 16 May and grew in response to events. Originally intended as a pamphlet, the first book length draft was finished on 14 June, the day that white flags were reported over Port Stanley. My concern was not with the fighting but with why Britain went to war when it need not have—the ease with which this was done, and the lack of serious political opposition. I have not tried to establish what motivated Margaret Thatcher on a day-to-day basis, therefore, although such a history would be valuable. Rather, I have tried to explore the political culture that generated the war on the British side. My hope is that this might encourage people in the UK to make it more difficult next time.

Although I have criticized Argentina's own aggressive policy in its international context, I have not presumed to analyse its domestic politics. I am happy to leave to others the important work of exposing the Junta's role.

Most of *Iron Britannia* appeared as the special August issue of *New Left Review*. I would like to thank, individually and collectively, all of my fellow editors for their rapid and supportive response to the first draft. In particular, Robin Blackburn encouraged me to embark upon the project and suggested many valuable ideas; Fred Halliday made detailed and effective written comments, and, above all, Mike Davis edited the text with enthusiasm, improved it throughout and shared the final, white nights of preparation.

This edition contains a new chapter (No 5) with some reflections on the nature of public and media support for the war. Along with various small changes I have also added some paragraphs to the discussion on Thatcherism and to the penultimate section on the issues of principle raised by the conflict. If, before embarking, the reader wants to know what my 'position' is on the Falklands, he or she should glance through that chapter (No 7).

I have been very fortunate to benefit from the advice and encouragement of Neil Belton, John Berger, Hugh Brody, Peter Fuller, Andrew Gamble, Judith Herrin and Frances Walsh. The Transnational Institute has supported me patiently and generously, it gives me great pleasure to be able to thank it publicly. Finally, I am grateful to the publishers who said 'Yes, quick'.

A book written in haste is certain to contain errors, for which I am entirely to blame. However, I hope that the reader will not be too annoyed. I enjoyed writing *Iron Britannia* and would like it to be read for pleasure.

21 August 1982

For Eleanor and Tamara Deutscher,
who made me see that it was not a comic expedition.

Chronology

April 2 Argentina seizes the Falkland Islands.

3 House of Commons holds special Saturday debate.

4 Argentinian force captures South Georgia.

5 Lord Carrington resigns as Foreign Secretary, HMS *Hermes* and HMS *Invincible* sail from Portsmouth to head Task Force.

6 UK says no negotiated solution without total Argentinian withdrawal. Second Parliamentary debate, Tony Benn demands return of Task Force. EEC applies sanctions.

7 UK announces 200 mile exclusion zone around the Islands from 12 April.

8 US Secretary of State General Haig arrives in London to attempt a mediating peace shuttle.

12 Haig returns to London after round trip to Buenos Aires. Blockade goes into force.

13 Haig returns to Washington, Junta appeals to UN.

14 Third Parliamentary debate, Michael Foot continues to endorse Task Force.

16 Transcript of conversation between Reagan and Haig leaked in which the US President says that 'Maggie wants a skirmish'.

19 Task Force off Ascension island, grows massively with reinforcements. Thatcher rejects Junta's peace plan.

25 British forces re-capture South Georgia.

26 UN Secretary General says Resolution 502 applies to UK as well as Argentina.

27 Foot calls on Thatcher to accept the UN peace call.

29 UK announces total air-exclusion zone over Falklands, Argentina announces its own counter-blockade.

30 Reagan announces that US will support Britain, confirming failure of Haig Mission, as Peruvian initiative begins.

May 1 British bomb Port Stanley airstrip, first air clashes (3 Argentinian planes downed). Peruvian peace initiative said to be acceptable.

2 British nuclear submarine *Conqueror* sinks *General Belgrano* outside the exclusion zone and at least 200 miles from Task Force. Over 300 Argentinian sailors killed. Peruvian peace initiative fails.

3 British helicopters attack two Argentinian patrol ships.

4 HMS *Sheffield* sunk by Exocet missile, a Harrier shot down.

7 Britain extends its exclusion zone to 12 miles off Argentina's coast.

12 QE 2 sails from Portsmouth as troopship; arguments in UK over role of media and government, right-wing condemns war criticism.

15 British commando attack on Pebble Island.

16 EEC renews its sanctions against Argentina.

18 EEC imposes increase in farm prices on UK, over-riding Britain's 'veto'.

20 Final House of Commons debate on eve of landing. 33 MPs vote against use of the Task Force.

21 Task Force lands over 1,000 British troops at San Carlos unopposed and begins to consolidate its bridgehead; strength increases to 5,000.

22 Argentinian Air Force begins to sink British ships in intense bombing runs.

28 Goose Green taken by British forces. Pope arrives in the UK.

June 3 British call on Argentinian garrison at Port Stanley to surrender. Tories win Mitcham and Morden by-election.

7 Reagan arrives in London on way to Paris summit.

8 Heavy British losses at Bluff Cove (50 killed).

11 Pope arrives in Buenos Aires.

14 Ceasefire arranged as Argentinians in Port Stanley surrender.

'I had the winter at the back of my mind. *The winter*. What will the winter do? The wind, the cold. Down in South Georgia the ice, what will it do? It beat Napoleon at Moscow.'

(Margaret Thatcher, *Daily Express*, 26 July 1982)

1 Glare of War

WHEN HISTORY repeats itself, the first time is tragedy, the second farce. Despite its Marxist origin, the aphorism is now a received wisdom. Perhaps that alone is good reason to abandon the idea. Certainly we have gone beyond it. The British recapture of the Falkland Islands was obviously a repeat performance, although there is argument over precisely what was taking place again. It reminded some of the original eviction of Argentina by an English fleet in 1833, while Trevor-Roper compared it to the even earlier confrontation with Spain over the islands in 1770. The most apt and widely drawn comparison however, has been with the Suez crisis of 1956. Indeed, when the British Parliament gathered on 3 April 1982 for a special Saturday debate on Argentina's invasion, readers of that morning's *Times* were told: 'The emergency sitting of the Commons will be the first on a Saturday since 3 November 1956, over Suez.' Yet the 1956 Anglo-French invasion of Egypt was itself a clownish attempt by the two European powers to recreate their colonial domination over the Suez Canal. Today, therefore, British history has entered a new stage. We are witnesses to the repeat of a repeat, and as befits the late modern world it was played out on television and in the press. If the first time is tragedy and the second farce, the third is spectacle: the media event that was launched when the British fleet set sail for the South Atlantic.

Will reality and spectacle eventually collide? It was remarkable how well the British public relations side of the Falklands affair stood up. It was helped, of course, by a quick and, in part, fortuitous victory. Nonetheless, the manipulation of opinion was at least as masterful (and as important) as the military operation. Initially a clear majority wanted to see no loss of life and, for some weeks after the Task Force had sailed, held that the Falklands were not worth a single British death. Yet 256 were killed on the British side, along with three Falklanders, and 777 wounded. Argentina suffered at least 1,800 dead, missing and injured.[1] This casualty list was found acceptable. It was even seen as agreeably 'light', given the intensity of the combat. The figures were glossed as a measure of British military prowess, for being so *low*. But they were based on a gross miscalculation, not of the incompetence of Argentina's army—in which British estimates that it would fail to perform proved accurate—but in the persistence of its air force, predicted in the House of Commons by Tam Dalyell, a critic of the expedition. Indeed, if the 'profusion' of unexploded Argentine bombs had gone off, the story might have had another ending. Despite the skill of the British operation, 'it would have been impossible to continue', one officer commented, had the enemy ordnance been correctly fused.[2] Yet the British got away with it and now see this as a demonstration of their virtue. Britannia never shows remorse.

But if the British Government managed to 'wrap up' the Falklands War, and then to issue it on video, something else has been unwrapped in the process. For all the talk of truth being the first casualty of war, the Gothic excesses of conflict may clarify, especially as they bring domestic forces to a head. The glare of war can illuminate darkness just as the flash of lightning at night can reveal a white image of the surrounding landscape. When the darkness sets in again and the thunder rolls on, those who love the spectacle will talk about the lightning. I am interested in what it showed: in particular, what the Falklands war can tell us about Britain today.

In the postwar years, when a welfare state of sorts was built in Britain and even pioneered in some respects, the country's image was of a society in social peace. True, this was disturbed by poor industrial relations at times. But mass unemployment was regarded as a thing of the past, not only because Keynesianism supposedly made it redundant, but also because unemployment would rend apart the special fabric of Britain's postwar consensus. In spite of all appearances, or indeed because of them, a classless sense of 'fair-play' was seen to preside over social relations within the UK. All loved the Queen, and the amusing antique ceremonies of monarchy thus unified classes and regions. The quiet sense of shared self-confidence was conjured up by the unarmed 'bobby'; the police were like uncles who kept a kindly eye out for understandable misdemeanours, crimes of passion and the very infrequent villain. There was no country like it.

It has never been clear to me what proportion of the population actually believed this vision they were all supposed to share. It was a 'worldview' of the United Kingdom generated domestically, rather than a reality at any time. Yet it was also more than public relations. Its projection needed sincerity more than cynicism, even if that sincerity was self-deceptive.

But who could hold such a view today as the essential attribute of 'Britishness'? The Falklands crisis coincided with the first anniversary of the death of Bobby Sands and the start of the campaign in which Thatcher linked the attitude of the government in Westminster directly to the death of prisoners in Northern

Ireland. Riots followed in June 1981 right across England (significantly omitting the major cities of Scotland and Wales). A reaction to the brutal policing of blacks especially, the riots saw the full deployment of hit-squads by the police and the first mainland use of CS gas. The notable behaviour of British football gangs in Europe could now be seen as an expression of the 'real' England, rather than a youthful exception to it. Today, the Falklands expedition has completed this transfer of the British image in the eyes of the world—from phlegmatic bobby to enthusiastic commando.

In one sense its timing was accidental, determined by the troubles of Argentina and the strains within its military Junta. In another, the whole thing could not have come at a more convenient moment for Thatcher. The Conservative Party's popularity, although recovering somewhat from a winter nadir, remained stubbornly low. The only bright spot on the horizon for Tory prospects was the intense division of opinion within the Labour Party that made it seem an improbable alternative. At the same time both the main parties were confronted by the liquidation of their duopoly. The rise of the Social Democrats in alliance with the Liberals threatens more than the usual challenge. For should they come even close to victory in the next election, proportional representation may be introduced and the structure and certainties of the old Parliamentary parties will be gone forever. After apparently faltering at the final gate, Roy Jenkins—the effective founder, 'statesman' and now leader of the SDP—won a critical Scottish by-election to return to the House of Commons at the end of March. Within days Galtieri's forces stormed Port Stanley.

The rise of the SDP, the fissures within the two main parties (the divisions amongst the Conservatives are less discussed but no less significant), the unprecedented volatility of the opinion polls, are all part of the general crisis in Britain—one now so protracted that the very word seems to induce a yawn. Perhaps indeed it is the work of sleepwalkers. Certainly most discussion of the British crisis is either ponderously beside the point or sensationally trivial, as attention is displaced away from the political centre.

Slowly, however, the perceived location of the crisis has moved in on the country's masters, while material conditions continue to degenerate. The regiments of the unemployed have grown much faster than even the military budget under Thatcher's direction: officially three million, actually around four million, and the numbers beginning to experience the long-term debilitation of being unwaged mounting even more sharply. By the same token—or lack of it—bankruptcies have reached a record: 5,500 in the first half of 1982, a 75% rise on 1981. During the three months of the Falklands

War 226 companies went into liquidation every week, while a torrent of capital cascaded into overseas investments.[3]

The Falklands crisis was born of these circumstances. It joined the now venerable tradition of quack cures imbibed by the British political establishment in the hopes of a relatively painless solution to its woes. The media welcomed the dispatch of the task force with a zeal similar to its enthusiasms for anti-union legislation, entry into the Common Market, the advent of North Sea oil, or monetarism. (Perhaps the Falklands created a slightly greater spectrum between enthusiasm and scepticism than normal, but that was all.) In their time all these seemed marvellous ways to reverse Britain's decline without challenging the nature of sovereignty in the UK. After the Falklands victory, in a major speech at Cheltenham to which we shall return (reproduced in full in the Appendix, p. 149 below), Thatcher baptized 'the spirit of the South Atlantic', as the 'real spirit' of Britain. 'The spirit has stirred and the nation has begun to assert itself. Things are not going to be the same again ... Britain has ceased to be a nation in retreat.' In Thatcher's presentation, the long crisis is essentially over. Britain has been cured! In private, other politicians may scoff at such sleight of hand, while they envy the conviction with which it is played. Meanwhile, they and Thatcher share as a controlling vanity the belief that whatever else may be wrong with the UK, at least 'the British know how to rule'. Thatcher may seem to have challenged this idea with her assault on gentrified amateurs and her cult of professionalism. But both notions, of 'professionalism' and 'amateurism' alike, as used in British politics today, share the same presumption: that sovereignty is something that belongs to an elite by special right. The style of domination is in dispute and behind this there is a clash of interests, but no challenge to the received institutions of privilege. It is this which has made Thatcher's celebration of the Falklands War at one and the same time novel and conservative. She has given the Parliamentary nation a new expression, but she *has* expressed its longings and desires to escape from accumulated frustrations. She may have exploited the opportunity of the Falklands War, but it was pressed upon her by Parliament itself.

The key political event in the dispatch of the Task Force, which explains why it was sent into combat, and which itself must be explained if we are to seek the cause of the British response, was the behaviour of the House of Commons on 3 April. The day after the Falklands were overrun, Parliament sat for its special session. What happened then may have transformed the chemistry of British politics: it certainly injected onto it an odious stench that will take a long time to clear. In party political terms the outcome was quite remarkable. Previously Thatcher had represented the aggressive

18

wing of the Conservative Party and a definite minority within the country; harsh, even balmy, high on monetaristic evangelism. Espousing the need for home-spun discipline, she stood for short, sharp government. Because she seemed to know what she was doing and what needed to be done, amidst dishevelled political alternatives who appeared to betray their confusion and incompetence, Thatcher retained a support much wider than her band of true followers. Yet she remained an extremist in a country that has always cultivated the worship of moderation.

The Falklands debate changed that. The House of Commons overwhelmingly endorsed a gesture of military determination to salvage a national humiliation. As *The Times* put it, it was just like the Second World War when we went in to save the Poles. Except that there remains a difference between 1939 and today: the Poles were Poles, but the Falklanders are British![4] To listen to that Parliamentary debate on the radio was to enter into a kind of collective inanity, in which each speaker held up a distorting mirror for the others to admire themselves in—it was a self-consciously historic occasion.

It made Thatcher no longer the political outrider. She had come to power through a double Party crisis: the complacency of Labour under Callaghan allowed the Tories to win the 1979 election, while Thatcher herself had grabbed the Conservative leadership after Heath's demoralizing defeat in 1974. Though no longer an intruder, she remained a misfit until the 3 April debate elevated her into the war leader of a bi-partisan consensus. Or rather a multi-party unanimity, for Liberals and the SDP also spoke out vehemently against the nation's suffering at the crunch of Argentina's heel. Thatcher's new role only became clear after the debate, as the fleet set sail. It was her navy. (The Queen's yacht *Britannia* was not dispatched even though it is especially equipped to be turned into a hospital ship in times of war.) During the debate itself, Thatcher and her government were rebuked by the House for having allowed the debacle on the islands to occur in the first place. She was shamed, yet she was also dared, even taunted into action, in particular by Enoch Powell:

> The Prime Minister, shortly after she came into office, received the soubriquet as the 'Iron Lady'. It arose in context of remarks which she made about defence against the Soviet Union and its allies. But there was no reason to suppose that the Right Honourable Lady did not welcome and, indeed, take great pride in that description. In the next week or two this House, the nation and the Right Honourable Lady herself will learn of what metal she is made.

Apparently Thatcher nodded her head in agreement. Michael Foot was less personal but delivered just as strong a challenge. The

House, the country, was 'paramountly concerned', he stated,

> about what we can do to protect those who rightly and naturally look to us for protection. So far they have been betrayed. The Government must now prove by deeds—they will never be able to do it by words—that they are not responsible for the betrayal and cannot be faced with that charge.

'The Government must now prove by deeds ...' By speaking thus Foot made himself the voice of the House of Commons that day. He was the spokesperson for its fervid assent to the expedition. The Tory Party—especially its right-wing—was suckled and drew comfort from his oratory; the Liberals were out-liberaled by his appeals to the small nations of the world; the SDP was shown what social democracy was all about; the Labour Party could look with pride upon its leader, he was better than Denis Healey after all. With morale all of a crumble on the Tory frontbench, it was Foot who gave true leadership. As he sat down, Edward du Cann, a leading Conservative back-bencher, rose to congratulate him:

> There are times in the affairs of our nation when the House should speak with a single, united voice. This is just such a time. The Leader of the Opposition spoke for us all. He did this nation a service when, in clear and unmistakable terms, he condemned what he called this brutal aggression and when he affirmed the rights of the Falkland Islanders to decide their own destiny.

Yes, Foot was Churchill and Foot was Bevan, rolled into one. He was the John Bull of the Labour movement, the world statesman confronted by the forces of evil; righteous and determined he spoke for the whole, united House. Foot called for action. Thatcher carried it out. He delivered the country into her hands.

Naturally Thatcher was obliged to do something if only to secure her own back-bench support. She had already announced that a task force was in preparation. Yet she did so with nervousness rather than self-confidence at the beginning of the debate. After Foot's demand, it became instead an Armada sailing at the behest of the House with the Prime Minister at the helm: the Commons nationalized Thatcher's style of leadership—it was an Iron Britannia that emerged.

Why did this take place? A key reason is the national and institutional place of Parliament itself and the false history which it gives to the ruling parties. When the House of Commons was bombed during the last world war, Churchill insisted that it be rebuilt to exactly the old specifications, as a stuffy chamber without desks. It remains today an artificially reconstructed club that has never taken the measure of its collapse from being the seat of Empire and arbiter of world history, so that it appears to us today like a political institution from the age of dinosaurs. A monstrous beast, capable of great noise and immeasurable consumption of putrid vegetable matter, it believes that it has been chosen to dominate the surface of the globe, yet it has a disproportionately tiny brain.

In the House of Commons today, usually irrelevant and empty dramas are acted out in an anachronistic language. This has led many to think that it is no longer important and that power has passed to other places and circles. Not at all. Parliament is the seat of British sovereignty, especially in matters of war and peace, with which sovereignty is so directly connected. Parliament proved this on 3 April. Its frothing and raging were all the purer for being brought about by an object as insignificant as the Falklands. The mated, mutual evocation of the principles of British sovereignty by the leaders of all parties led to the almost instant birth of the Task Force. Together they made a consensus of extremism. Michael Foot has written in praise of Disraeli for refusing to 'bow to the House of Commons in one of those swelling tempers when it converts itself into a mob'.[5] On 3 April 1982, it was Foot himself who became the leader of the pack.

Doubtless it is not simply the institution of Parliament alone which is to blame. The law courts with their archaic distinctions; the Oxbridge system; the feebleness of the civil service; the font of 'excellence' in Britain, the public school system—these are all part and parcel of the ruling arch, but one in which Parliament is the keystone. How can one describe the extraordinary influence of this political culture? Little incidents capture its flavour more than anything. In mid-May I had reason to talk to a stranger in Trafalgar Square. I wanted to ask him about the number of a bus which had gone by. He was a friendly looking man, probably in his 50s, with a moustache and a stiff white collar, smoking an excellent cigar. So I asked him about the latest news from the South Atlantic, and then his opinion of the matter. 'It's *noblesse oblige* really, don't you think? *Noblesse oblige*. Otherwise we wouldn't be able to hold our head up high in the world'. I pointed out that they might sink the Queen Elizabeth, which would not do much for our world standing. He agreed that was the risk we had to run. It wasn't jingoism. It wasn't said with any love of battle. There wasn't any hatred of dagoes. Duty demanded it. We parted with a cheerio.

The attitude he expressed would seem as warm, as understandable and as irrelevant as the reminiscence of an immigrant grandfather about the Russo-Japanese war. It was not a chance encounter, in that the majority of those who think of themselves as members of a ruling elite in Britain share his wavelength. The only important qualification to add is that they remain skilful enough to stifle, if not silence completely, those voices which are radically different. Evidence of this during the Falklands crisis was the way the *Financial Times* appeared to be a straggler in the wilderness. It was unable to condemn the government unequivocally, yet all its reason told it that the affair was absurd. The bourgeois rationality of capital, or, if that sounds too heavy, the plain calculation of good business, was almost unbearably self-evident. The Falklands were hardly worth a toss. It would be necessary to protect the way of life of its British community, of course, because how else could one be sure of safeguards for foreign business communities in Argentina or elsewhere? But the issue of sovereignty-and-righteousness could not be taken seriously in the absence of *any* definable substance, especially when it put at risk the very considerable interests of the City and British capital in Argentina and Latin America generally.

Yet in the House of Commons it was seen exactly the other way around. The invasion of the Falklands was nothing *but* an infringement of its dominion. Therefore, oddly enough, Argentina's action was completely and overwhelmingly an assault upon British rule itself: the House of Commons and the Crown. It was not just the insult of having one's small toe pinched by a Third World upstart that was humiliating. Because successive Governments had been trying to rid themselves of the islands and secure a closer relationship with Buenos Aires, because nobody in the Commons actually cared very much if at all about the islanders, because they were anyway so few in number that they could easily have been given munificent compensation—a point we will come to in a moment—because, in other words, there *were* no interests involved, it was purely a matter of spirit. Britain's 'standing' in the world was at stake. This was everything! Nothing real was being contested, therefore that most dangerously unreal aspect of international relations was at risk, the very aura of sovereignty itself, the sacred cow of the world order: *credibility*.

Each party, feeling the domestic crisis breathing down its neck, rallied in its own way to the call of history and the nation's 'honour'. Some leapt for joy, others scurried, many panted to catch up, plenty caught the whiff of intimidation, the job was done: the MPs had rallied to the flag. Only a despised 5% of them, mainly from the Labour left managed some co-ordinated dissent later in the war.[6] They were quite unable to make any impact on the crucial first day when it began. One of them, Tam Dalyell, has argued that this was all due to chance and that if the invasion had taken place on a Thursday, say, rather than a Friday when MPs were dispersed, then wiser councils would have prevailed—especially his own on the response of the Labour front-bench.[7] This is implausible, but Dalyell is right to stress that the role of Labour was crucial in the affair. He goes so far as to say that had Thatcher not known in advance that Labour would call for 'deeds', she would not have announced the sending of the fleet. But even if she had, it could not have been sent into combat without the initial unity of Parliament.

Dalyell's account of the 3 April debate is especially interesting in one respect. The leaders of the House colluded to ensure that it was kept brief. The Commons assembled for the special Saturday session to set the country's face to war and adjourned after a mere three hours, during which the opening and closing speeches of the four front-bench speakers took nearly an hour and a half. Yet an attempt by one MP to have the time extended to five hours, so that more opinions could be heard, was voted down by the MPs themselves. The real judgement of such a collective is revealed precisely in adversity, when its response to a crisis matters. The combination of instinct, collaboration and procedure defined the true methods of British parliamentary rule.

The united House of Commons ensured a 'united nation' prepared to go into battle. As Peter Jenkins put it, it was not Thatcher's war but 'Parliament's war', because of this.[8] It is therefore necessary, if we are to inquire into our rulers' capacity for dangerous folly, to examine the construction of this unity itself. And while it was a British occasion on 3 April, other states armed like the United Kingdom with nuclear weapons, are just as capable of their own demonstrations of sovereign pride. I will look at each of the speeches made during the great debate on that day, a fascinating compendium. What does the 'true spirit' of the nation actually look and feel like? How does Great Britain go to war? Is this indeed the renaissance of a democracy discovering the virtues of firmness in a just cause? Is this the bedrock *health* of Britain? Or rather, when we look upon the proceedings of a united House of Commons do we find ourselves in the presence of the British disease itself?

2   The Crackpot Parliament

'I slightly bridle when the word 'democracy' is applied to the United Kingdom. Instead of that I say, 'we are a Parliamentary nation'. If you ... put us into the jar labelled 'Democracy', I can't complain: I can only tell you that you have understood very little about the United Kingdom.'

(Enoch Powell, interviewed in *The Guardian*, 15 June 1982)

BEFORE WE examine the specific contributions to the assemblage of 'national unity' invoked on 3 April, some background information is essential. The British went to war in a welter of fine words about protecting the right of peoples to 'self-determination', and the need to repel aggression so as to ensure that it does not 'pay'. Hardly a word of this was meant by those who actually insisted upon a military consummation. For a start, they sank the *General Belgrano* quite illegally, which unleashed the real fighting war. The importance of these questions is considerable only because a great number of people who were not directly involved took them seriously. So I will discuss them towards the end of this essay, as principles in their own right. But in order to follow what happened in Parliament on 3 April, the questions posed by the specific, ambiguous status of the Falkland Islands should be registered.

Historically, it transpires that British officials have long had doubts as to the legitimacy of their country's claim to the Falklands. In 1910 Foreign Office memos thought Argentina's claim 'not altogether unjustified'. In the 1930s some kind of transfer of sovereignty was considered. In 1940 a file was titled, 'Proposed offer by HMG to reunite Falkland Islands with Argentina and acceptance of lease'. (The *Sunday Times* analysis emphasizes the word 'reunite'). In 1946 a UK internal research paper described the British seizure of the Islands in 1833 as an 'act of unjustified aggression'.[1] Since 1965, when Argentina raised the issue at the United Nations, London and Buenos Aires have been negotiating. According to the *Economist*, 'the Argentines were encouraged to pursue a negotiated settlement by the fact that almost every British minister with whom they dealt came to recognize at least the *de facto* force of their claim'.[2]

What was the substance of this 'recognition'? It was perhaps summed up in a still confidential report by Labour's Ted Rowlands who visited the Falklands on behalf of the Callaghan government in

1977. His conclusion was 'keep British sovereignty over the islanders, but give Argentina sovereignty over the territory'. It was 'the people, not the land itself' which seemed to him to constitute the crucial issue.[3] This distinction was met by a 'leaseback' proposal in which sovereignty would be granted to Argentina while government control remained in the hands of Britain. Rowlands's successor in the Thatcher administration was Nicholas Ridley who continued to pursue such a settlement. But before he went out to the Falklands in 1980 to consult the islanders, he was apparently subjected to a 'fearful mauling' for his ideas by the Prime Minister. Denied a clear mandate and restricted to presenting the leaseback idea as a mere 'option', the fate of Ridley's mission was predictable: 'The younger and more cosmopolitan islanders tended to be sympathetic to some accommodation with Argentina; and the view was that between a third and a *half* of the 1,800 population might have accepted some form of leaseback. Islanders of this persuasion argue that, had Mr Ridley come down with a firm announcement that the islanders had now to rethink their future, that the British were seeking leaseback and would compensate any islander who wanted to leave, the mood might have been more constructive. But Mr Ridley had been given no such mandate by the Cabinet'.[4]

We can therefore discern both a main current of British policy and an undercurrent pulling against it. The major thrust was to achieve a settlement that protected the *lives* of the resident people while assigning formal *sovereignty* of the terrain to Argentina. The undertow was primarily a Tory intransigence, shared by Thatcher, that played up the islanders' additional wish to 'remain British' and ran counter to their evident best interests, and even the desires of many or perhaps *most* of them.

Argentina meanwhile tried to woo the islanders. The 'Malvinas' could become 'the most pampered region' of the country if they joined it, and Argentinian officials specifically offered 'a democratic form of government, a different legal system, different customs, a different form of education. The only thing they wanted was sovereignty'.[5] It will help to bear these facts in mind when considering the response of British political classes to the Falklands crisis. Labour and Conservative governments had been striving to ensure that local law and administration remained 'British' and in the hands of the inhabitants while conceding sovereignty.

A major determinant in this apparent convergence towards a diplomatic solution was the economic and demographic decline of the Falklands community. In this context the final, impetuous Argentinian decision to launch a surprise invasion looks stupid, quite apart from being wrong. It is not inconceivable that political opposition on the Islands could simply have been bought out. Before the invasion, one farm manager reckoned that his farmhands would have left the Islands for £10,000.[6] It seems that had they actually been offered this amount by Buenos Aires—or £20,000 or £50,000—most of the locally-born Islanders would have willingly followed the trail to New Zealand and elsewhere, already taken by a third of the population (and an increasing proportion of the young) since 1945. At an infinitesimal fraction of the eventual human and economic cost of the war, a combination of local self-government and generous compensation for emigration could have peacefully removed Britain's 'social base' from the Falklands.

Instead, the Junta ordered an invasion. After the takeover, play was made in the British press about how the islanders had been forced to drive on the right instead of the left, and how those who refused to submit to this instruction bravely created bottlenecks for Argentinian troopcarriers. There are twelve miles of metalled road on the Falklands. The Junta instructed its forces to 'respect' the inhabitants. None of them or the small British garrison were killed in the invasion. On the day of the takeover, Galtieri stated that there would be 'no disruption' in the lives of the islanders. He also asked for an 'honourable agreement' with the UK.[7] After the British reconquest, it was reported that Port Stanley was 'in much better shape than one might have expected'. Many untended homes had not been vandalized. The local people had been 'largely ignored' by the invaders.[8] Snobbish to the end, the Junta had treated the inhabitants with the velvet glove traditionally applied to its country's privileged European settlements, rather than the brutal knuckleduster applied to the workers of Cordoba or the Indians in Tucuman province.

Against this, the line which Thatcher took was that British people were being subjected to intolerable oppression. In one interview she claimed that the islanders had been having a 'marvellous life' until they were invaded by thousands of soldiers of 'an alien creed'.[9] The implication was that the Junta was trying to take over *the people* and reduce them to the oppressed status of its own citizenry. A similar argument was pursued by Noel Annan in his apologia for Thatcher in the *New York Review of Books*.[10] Somehow or other it seems that if we are not willing to countenance the use of war to free the Falklanders from their plight, then we have not learnt the lessons of the fate of the Jews in central Europe.

Only one aspect of this argument, if it can be so described, is potentially valid. The Junta are a lying and murderous lot who cannot be trusted. If a Falklander wanted to speak out against their methods or to demand parliamentary democracy in Buenos Aires, he or she could have been summarily rounded up. Thus it was right to demand that Argentina's forces be withdrawn and that independent protection of the islanders' civil rights be ensured. Sovereignty should have been ceded to Argentina, not for the nationalist reasons that it has advanced, but for the practical ones British officials of left and right had already deemed sensible (I will return to this issue in Chapter 7). At the same time the local government of those who desired to stay should have remained in their own hands. Given the Junta's basically pro-British feelings and their desire for an 'honourable' agreement, such an arrangement was not implausible, even without the use of economic sanctions.

However, even if we suppose the ridiculous and presume that the Junta really wanted to devour the souls of the islanders with its 'alien creed', would it then have been proper to use force? The answer is surely 'no' for at least two reasons. First, the territory of the Falklands should belong to Argentina anyway. Second, the numbers involved make such a proposition absurd. This is not accidental. As I also argue in Chapter 7, the tiny number of Falklanders makes any idea of their own political independence 'bloody ridiculous', to use the formulation of Harry Milne, the Stanley manager of the Falkland Islands Company.[11] So too the dispatch of the task force. The costs of the expedition have not yet been totted up but on the British side alone they will probably total between £1.5 and £2 billion. Every single local-born Falklander, man, woman and even child, could have been given compensation of £100,000 each and £10,000 a year per head for twenty years, and the costs would have been less than a tenth of the war and the projected cost of a garrison, leaving aside the grave loss of life. Money not arms was the solution.

There are today about 1,300 locally born inhabitants still on the islands.[12] They call themselves 'Kelpers' after the giant Kelp seaweed of the South Atlantic. It is not hard to detect a note of stoical disparagement of their own conditions in the term. Their society could only have improved with the 'pampering', stability and trade that would have accompanied the Argentinian flag. The Kelpers would have joined the privileged Anglo-Argentine community, not the 'disappeared ones', and could have retained all their rights as British subjects except for their subjugation to the House of Commons, had not that chamber decided, in its *own* egocentric interests, to go to war for the Falklands.

This applies with a special vengeance to Margaret Thatcher perhaps, but it also goes for the Labour leadership, which endorsed the need to 'liberate' the Falklands and restore freedom to the islands. Labour did support the deployment of the Task Force, but *even then*—as we are about to witness—it declined to make any distinction between the lives of the people and sovereignty over the territory. It thus reneged on its own approach to the issue when in office. Labour went out of its way to dismiss the offers of the Junta and to secure the fatal elision of land and inhabitants that made the struggle over the Falklands a primitive clash of national sovereignty between Britain and Argentina.

The fateful debate was opened by Thatcher. These were her first words:

> The House meets this Saturday to respond to a situation of great gravity. We are here because, for the first time for many years, British sovereign territory has been invaded by a foreign power.[13]

After describing the first information she had received, she went on:

> I am sure that the whole House will join me in condemning totally this unprovoked aggression by the Government of Argentina against British territory. (Honourable Members: 'Hear, hear'.) It has not a shred of justification, and not a scrap of legality.

She gave more details of takeover, then stated:

> I must tell the House that the Falkland Islands and their dependencies remain British territory. No aggression and no invasion can alter that simple fact. It is the Government's objective to see that the islands are freed from occupation and are returned to British administration at the earliest possible moment.

Thus the entire initial position taken by the Prime Minister was concerned with the issue of territorial sovereignty, not the islanders. There can be little doubt that this was a true expression of her feelings. What had been usurped for her was some*thing* that belonged to Britain. This was the primary, the national, fact. She then went on to deal with the secondary issue:

> Argentina has, of course, long disputed British sovereignty over the islands. We have absolutely no doubt about our sovereignty, which has been continuous since 1833. Nor have we any doubt about the unequivocal wishes of the Falkland Islanders, who are British in stock and tradition, and they wish to remain British in allegiance. We cannot allow the democratic rights of the islanders to be denied by the territorial ambitions of Argentina.

Two things are significant about this statement. First, as we have seen, there *was* in fact a consistent record of official British attempts in recent times to negotiate away sovereignty. Second, one can observe the wilful fashion in which the Prime Minister elided the territorial question with the democratic rights of the islanders. Consider, for instance, their 'British tradition', which never gave them a vote in the election of their own Governor or conferred UK citizenship. Thatcher demagogically made no attempt to distinguish the Kelpers' real traditions so as to seek their preservation; instead, she made the appointment from London of their local ruler the defining and definitive attribute of their way of life. Moreover, she proceeded to claim:

> Over the past 15 years, successive British Governments have held a series of meetings with the Argentine Government to discuss the dispute. In many of these meetings elected representatives of the islanders have taken part. We have always made it clear that their wishes were paramount and that there would be no change in sovereignty without their consent and without the wishes of the House.

This statement seems to have been false. To have held to it would have been the equivalent of the British Government asserting eternal sovereignty. And Thatcher was soon to back away from the 'paramountcy' of the islanders' desires during the period of diplomatic manoeuvering, only to reinstate it as a rhetorical imperative on the eve of victory. The important thing to note, therefore, is the *use* being made of the 'wishes' of the islanders, to justify London's claims.

Thatcher next tried to explain why no concrete steps had been taken to prevent an Argentinian take-over which had been forewarned weeks, if not months in advance. She was uncomfortably aware that in 1977 Callaghan had quietly dispatched a nuclear submarine and two frigates to the South Atlantic in a successful gamble to force the Junta back to the negotiating table after intelligence reports of a possible attack. This precedent placed Thatcher in a difficult partisan position and provided one of the key tensions of the debate. Her political image had been constructed around the projection of determination, resolution and iron fidelity to national defence—yet here the stereotypes were reversed. It was the ex-Labour Government, whose members were now sitting opposite, which could claim to have achieved all these things where she had failed. They had acted where she had deserted 'kith and kin'. Indeed, how could the embattled Labour front-bench, desperate for favourable publicity, possibly refrain from such an accusation when it caused Thatcher such pain?

The prospect was intolerable. Her reaction was to strike back and not only at Argentina. First she dredged up the case of South Thule. If you think that the Falklands are remote, try to find South Thule on the map. It is an uninhabitable dot close to the Antarctic below South Georgia. Thatcher claimed that it had been 'occupied' by Argentina in 1976 but that the traitors in the Labour Party did not even tell the House about this appalling transgression until 1978 (Buenos Aires had established a 'scientific' post there). She was interrupted by a questioner: surely South Thule was 'a piece of rock', there was 'a whole world of difference' between it and the 'imprisonment of 1,800 people' by Argentina. Not at all, answered Thatcher. 'We are talking about the sovereignty of British territory—which was infringed in 1976'. Although her efforts at baiting the opposition did not go down well in the chamber, the point was quite logical. It demonstrated the priorities to which she was attached. The sovereign territory might have well been no more than a lump knee-deep in bird droppings, all the same it was *our land*. A woman who puts millions out of work has no feeling for the life people lead. Rather, it is their abstract 'virtues' which stir her heart, as she made clear in her final sentences:

> The people of the Falkland Islands, like the people of the United Kingdom, are an island race. Their way of life is British; their allegiance is to the Crown. They are few in number but they have the right to live in peace, to choose their way of life, and to determine their own allegiance. Their way of life is British; their allegiance is to the Crown. It is the wish of the British people and the duty of Her Majesty's Government to do everything that we can to uphold that right. That will be our hope and our endeavour and, I believe, the resolve of every Member of the House.

There is no such thing as 'an island race' and it is most unlikely that Thatcher would speak in such laudatory tones about the Maltese or the Filipinos. But the thing to observe is the way the wishes of 'the people' have been used, by deliberate confusion, to stand in for the wishes of the Government in London. The right to live in peace, the right to choose one's own way of life, these are powerful and important—they refer to tranquillity, security, education, religion, language and jobs. The right to determine one's 'allegiance' is slightly different. (It has an odd, rather feudal ring, partly because it is not, 'the right of self-determination', i.e. statehood). To go on to say, 'Their way of life is British, their allegiance is to the Crown', is to fuse the attributes of their actual community existence with the Union Jack above their heads. It is to ignore, wilfully and deliberately, the possibility of distinguishing these two aspects, a practical possibility in this case because of the tiny numbers involved. When Thatcher stated that she already believed it to be the resolve of every member to give back to the Falklanders their 'rights', she was sending the hurricane of war to defend their 'right to live in peace'. It was *not* their lives she sought to defend, it was rather British sovereignty over them, and more generally 'Britishness' itself.

Michael Foot then rose and immediately made it clear in what way for Labour it was people not territory that mattered:

> The rights and the circumstances of the people in the Falkland Islands must be uppermost in our minds. There is no question in the

Falkland Islands of any colonial dependence or anything of the sort. It is a question of people who wish to be associated with this country [read: ruled by it] and who have built their whole lives on the basis of association with this country. We have a moral duty, a political duty and every other kind of duty [read: military] to ensure that that is sustained.

Here again it is possible to see how the islanders' lives were inextricably conflated with British rule over them, only this time under a cloud of moral purity. How damaging this stance was not only for Britain but for the islanders, was revealed in Foot's subsequent words:

The people of the Falkland Islands have the absolute right to look to us at this moment of their desperate plight, just as they have looked to us over the past 150 years. They are faced with an act of naked, unqualified aggression, carried out in the most shameful and disreputable circumstances. Any guarantee from this invading force is utterly worthless—as worthless as any of the guarantees that are given by this same Argentine Junta to its own people.

Note Foot's sweep as a historian, at home with the previous century-and-a-half in the most detailed way and also his characterization of 'unqualified aggression'. What he would have said if the Argentine forces had killed anyone can hardly be imagined. But what is most interesting here was his dismissal of the worth of any guarantees. This was his response to the offer made by Galtieri to let the Falklanders keep their own way of life (just as have many Welsh communities in Patagonia—as successfully, it could be added, as in many parts of Wales). Foot confused a 'guarantee' with a mere verbal promise, a conflation in which mental disorganization and deliberate misinterpretation seem to have been combined. Certainly to have taken the mere *word* of the Junta on trust would have been craven, but a 'guarantee' could mean international invigilation and enforcement. Here, perhaps, was a means of securing the islanders' way of life, and the withdrawal of Argentinian troops, and even a lucrative financial settlement. But—and this is the all-important point—Foot would not even allow such an option to be considered, let alone explored. Despite the lofty calibre of his words, he was no more concerned than Thatcher with the actual human lives involved. His interest was in a greater cause:

[to] uphold the rights of our country *throughout the world*, and the claim of our country to be a defender of people's freedom *throughout the world*, particularly those who look to us for special protection, as do the people in the Falkland Islands. (My emphasis.)

Foot then examined the conduct of the Thatcher Government,

pointedly contrasting its lack of foresight with Labour's prescience in 1977. This led him to the conclusion already quoted, that the Tories had 'betrayed' the islanders and now needed to 'prove by deeds' that they could make good their record. Because, Foot stressed, it was necessary after all to qualify our primary concern with the Falklanders themselves:

> *Even though* the position and the circumstances of the people who live in the Falkland Islands are uppermost in our minds—it would be outrageous if that were not the case—there is the longer term interest to ensure that foul and brutal aggression does not succeed in the world. If it does, there will be a danger not merely to the Falkland Islands, but to people all over this dangerous planet. (My emphasis.)

Now it is perfectly clear that as a result of the Falklands' expedition, small nations and good causes will not sleep easier in the world. How could those who desire a more just and less alarming planet wish more power to the likes of Margaret Thatcher? So far as Britain's 'particular' interests are concerned, as expressed by those who look to it for protection, Belize and British Guyana have been cited. The latter has a powerful neighbour, Venezuela, which claims a substantial part of its territory. Will the British response to the Falklands' seizure deter Venezuela more than would have an extended diplomatic campaign to ensure the community rights of the Kelpers? On the contrary. For instead of arming the politicians in Caracas with a powerful case to rein in their military, British reaction in the South Atlantic is just as likely to ensure an increase in the Venezuelan military budget. Exocet missiles and submarines will be added at great expense, funded by oil revenues. The greater the superiority achieved, the more likely it becomes that it will be used. This is so obvious that Michael Foot's motivation can hardly have been a real desire to ensure more peaceful relations internationally. But nor is it the case that he had radically changed his attitudes from the man who campaigned for British unilateral nuclear disarmament during the 1950s. There is an underlying continuity of attitude between the strand of opinion he belonged to then and his position on the Falklands crisis: the tradition of British liberalism.

It has long been remarked that the first CND campaign (1957-63) saw a renewal of the British liberal tradition of protest, that goes back to opposition to the slave trade. Humanitarian antagonism to the unnecessary and inhuman excesses of the world was the characteristic feature of this stance. It never challenged the system which produced such horrors and rather avoided any overall, systematic theory, for fear of dogmatism and ideological excess on its own part. Michael Foot is a contemporary embodiment of this tradition and exemplifies one of its most unpleasant aspects: its *moral imperialism*. For behind the presumption that a British voice must speak out against violations of humanity elsewhere (which is welcome), lies the assertion that the Anglo-Saxon accent can and should arbitrate across all frontiers. The globalism of the liberal conscience in this case is not a true internationalism. Despite its attractive aspects, its core is a presumption of national superiority. This was captured in the first CND campaign by one of the arguments for unilateralism: it would 'set an example for the world'. Britain would 'lead the way by its behaviour'. While a strand of English liberal moralism, then, was truly and properly appalled at the threat of mankind's absolute destruction in a nuclear exchange—and so protested against the infamous prospect of our genocide—another strand expressed the specific sense of national impotence. No longer a great power, subject to the fateful decisions of Washington and Moscow, Britain which had supposedly 'won the war' found it had lost any power to arbitrate the peace. The fate of the world was slipping inexorably from London's hands. Only a magnificent gesture, while some power to deflect events remained, could ensure a permanent legacy of influence.

Foot's sentiments over the Falklands are an archetypal expression of this liberal imperialism. The people are 'uppermost' in his mind, so far 'up' as to be out of sight, it transpires, while it is the 'longer-term' question that predominates. 'Foul and brutal aggression', that led to no loss of life amongst those aggressed, requires that the planet itself be policed against further danger. This is often the rallying cry of the metropolis as it seeks to maintain a world order. American officials justified their intervention in Vietnam on the same grounds; was not the 'domino theory' merely a more regional specification of the dangers of 'global example' espoused by Foot?[14]

How did Foot defend himself, when he came under criticism? In response to an open letter from Anthony Arblaster in *Tribune*, Foot argued that he had been assailed without any mention of the United Nations.[15] Its Charter is the 'centrepiece' of Labour's case, he wrote. 'Everything I have said has been governed by Labour's allegiance to the Charter.' The 'future prospects for peace throughout the world' as well as 'Labour's reputation', depended upon the Party honouring its international responsibility to the UN. In his view, the difference between the Suez and Falklands crises is that in the Falklands, Britain has acted 'in conformity with our United Nations obligations'. The argument is spurious. International opinion almost uniformly regards the squabble between the UK and Argentina as about national pride, while allegiance to the UN does not imply that Britain had to counter-attack the Junta's forces. Resolution 502 which called for the immediate withdrawal of

Argentine forces also called on both sides to resolve their differences diplomatically and demanded 'an immediate cessation of hostilities'. Furthermore Article 51 hardly extends the right of *self-*defence to non-national, dependent territories 7,000 miles away, whose sovereignty has already been placed on the negotiating table by the 'defending' country.[16]

Perhaps because he sensed the weakness of his appeal to trans-national legalism, Foot concluded his defence by tarnishing his once notable anti-fascist record. He drew a parallel with the Spanish Civil War. Thatcher, it seems, was leading the Republican side against a Franco-like invasion. Just as *Tribune* had done nothing to give aid and comfort to Franco in the thirties, so it should now abominate any support for General Galtieri, instead of demanding the recall of the Task Force. (Funny that Labour had sold many arms to the Argentine Junta.) Eric Heffer, an ambitious Labour leftist, equally endorsed Thatcher's response because, 'The Labour Party cannot agree to a bunch of fascist military thugs being allowed to do just what they like'. Nobody had suggested that they should. Just as Galtieri's claim that he is dedicated to the struggle against colonialism is nothing more than the mirror image in hypocrisy to Thatcher's assertion that she must defend the Falklanders' 'right to self-determination', so Foot's or Heffer's declaration that the Falklands War is a struggle against fascism also twins the Junta's demagogy.

It is necessary to leave the squabble in Labour's ranks to return to the less elastic mentality of the Conservative MPs. Michael Foot was followed in the debate by Edward du Cann, a great oak in the Tory bramble patch. As I've already noted, he immediately thanked Foot (one almost writes 'Sir Michael') for the way he 'spoke for us all'. The issue was straightforward, du Cann continued:

> Let us declare and resolve that our duty now is to repossess our possessions and to rescue our own people. [Note the order.] Our right to the Falkland Islands is undoubted. Our sovereignty is unimpeachable. British interest in that part of the world, in my judgement, is substantial. It is substantial in the Falklands Islands, however trivial the figures may appear to be. It is substantial in the sea, which has yet to yield up its *treasures*. It is also substantial in Antarctica. (My emphasis.)

Is that why *our* boys have gone to die? To protect *our* treasures in the Antarctic bleakness? Our companies will be able to yield it up. They will not be subject to our domestic rates of taxation, for it is a long way to the South Atlantic and we must be reasonable. Nonetheless, 'we' will be able to invest the profits abroad where they can earn 'us' the best rate of return. Thatcher's government is particularly splendid in this respect. For example, in the first two years of her administration, the outflow of capital after she lifted all exchange controls, came to £8,600,000,000. That is a substantial British interest deposited overseas. How could these, 'our' possessions, be safe, if we did not fight for them when necessary? Du Cann continued on another note:

> In the United Kingdom, we must accept reality. For all our alliances and for all the social politenesses which the diplomats so often mistake for trust, in the end in life it is self-reliance and only self-reliance that counts .... We have one duty only, which we owe to ourselves—the duty to rescue our people and to uphold our rights. Let that be the unanimous and clear resolve of the House this day. Let us hear no more about logistics—how difficult it is to travel long distances. I do not remember the Duke of Wellington whining about Torres Vedrás. (Honourable Members: 'Hear, hear'.) We have nothing to lose now except our honour. [Oh yes, and those substantial interests mentioned earlier.]

With the exception of my impertinent parenthesis, that was how du Cann concluded his historic intervention, adding that he was sure the nation's honour 'was safe in the hands of my honourable friend', a reference to Thatcher, both accolade and threat. It is ironic to compare the ravings of du Cann with the available thoughts of Mao Tse-tung. Self-reliance is one common theme. Voluntarism is another, Mao's attitude to moving mountains was similar to du Cann's on distance. Equally, for Mao 'every Communist must grasp the truth, "Political power grows out of the barrel of a gun" '. For du Cann, it seems, Mao's reality is one the United Kingdom must accept.

This Chinese parallel may seem far fetched, yet it recurs. In its post-victory editorial, for example, the *Economist* celebrated the Falklands War because 'Britain has long needed its own sort of cultural revolution'.[17] This ideological uplift is badly needed in the UK and America, it goes on to argue, because those under fifty regard military values as a bit of a joke. The Cultural Revolution itself, of course, initially placed the People's Army and its barracks version of Maoism in command of Chinese civilian life. A world away from Thatcherism, but is it accidental that the civilizations of countries that were once great empires and are now second-rank powers should foster similar longings?

Du Cann was followed by Enoch Powell. Powell was a monetarist before monetarism, a man of race before the race question. He was dismissed from the Conservative front bench by Heath, he left the Tory Party over the Common Market, and he now represents a Northern Ireland seat as a Unionist MP. He holds Margaret

Thatcher in his thrall. Powell began on an Ulster note. He demanded that proposals concerning the future of Northern Ireland, that were going to be presented to the Commons on the Monday, should be withdrawn. He regarded the Irish policy under development as designed to detach the North from the UK, in collusion with the southern Republic. Although his request was not echoed subsequently, the issue certainly explains part of the Tory venom over the Falklands. For after more than a decade of wearisome fighting and huge expense, Powell feared that London was beginning to consider the abandonment of Ulster. There too, a majority of the population wishes to remain 'British'. As every politican and journalist who has listened to Ian Paisley knows, those who follow his Orangeman's pipe and drum are Irish. Yet the Protestant Irish say they are British, and they fly the Union Jack with a fervid passion that can only be found in such places as Gibraltar and … the Falklands. Hence a central aspect of British politics is associated with the 'right' of the Falklanders to stay governed by the Crown. They do not seek self-determination and their land is claimed by another state—Argentina—just as the Irish Republic claims the North. Give way in the South Atlantic, and the position of the Ulstermen becomes more precarious. The integrity of the nation itself—the United Kingdom of Great Britain and Northern Ireland—might be threatened. Thus on the British side the Falklands War had an Orange pigmentation that the rest of the world largely failed to perceive.

Powell went on to demand the court martial of the handful of Royal Marines who surrendered to the larger Argentine invasion force the previous day, because the Secretary of State for Defence had commented in an interview that 'no British soldier ever surrenders'. Evidently, therefore, they had disobeyed orders and brought 'infamy to this country'. (Both he and the Secretary seemed to have forgotten Singapore.) Fortunately, Powell's amnesia was only partial. He was able to pluck out of his memory the wonderful coincidence that the 'Invincible' was the name of the capital ship in the British naval force that sank Von Spee's flotilla in a famous battle off the Falklands in December 1914. This was the example the Government should follow:

> There is only one reaction which is fit to meet unprovoked aggression upon one's own sovereign territory: that is direct and unqualified and immediate willingness—not merely willingness, but willingness expressed by action—to use force. The Government have set in train measures which will enable them to do that; but there must be nothing which casts doubt upon their will and their intention to do it.

He then went on to emphasize that the country would now see

whether Thatcher was indeed the 'Iron Lady'.

Powell was followed by Sir Nigel Fisher, a pillar of centrist Tory orthodoxy. His intervention struck a marginally new note. He seemed to suggest that there was probably little the Government could do: 'Britain has been humiliated. What can now be done? One's natural instinct is to get the invaders out, but it is much easier said than done.' Perhaps Argentina could be excluded from the World Cup. In Fisher's view,

> Whatever action is decided upon, this is a deeply depressing and distressing episode. We have failed—and failed lamentably—to defend the integrity of one of Britain's few remaining colonies.

No expense should be spared for the Task Force. The only possible excuse for the Government was that Ministers did not know that the invasion was a 'possibility'. Even that would not be very good. Fisher compared the Argentine *fait accompli* to the Nazi seizure of Norway in 1940. That, he pointed out, led to the fall of Chamberlain. It was quite a heavy number from a back-bencher with a handle to address to his own front-bench. One felt the call of his nostalgia: 'one of the few remaining colonies', as if this was a rare species the state had a duty to protect if only to prevent its extinction.

It was next the turn of Dr David Owen, who spoke for the new 'mould-breakers', the Social Democratic Party. The SDP was created to inject a European, bourgeois sense of proportion into the country's politics, a rather radical ambition as one can see. On this issue however, the SDP was itself completely shaped by the received conventions. The past was too heavy for the SDP at the vital moment when it had an opportunity to break away from Westminster's dormitory consciousness. Owen was Foreign Minister in Callaghan's Labour Government, which had 'saved' the Falklands in 1977 through preemptive naval deployment. He generously told the House about his own heroic role. Furthermore, his constituency is Plymouth, whence Drake set out against the Spanish in 1588.

> The Government have the right to ask both sides of the House for the fullest support in their resolve to return the Falkland Islands and the freedom of the islanders to British sovereignty.

Dr Owen cultivates his youthful looks and his open, non-ideological style. Perhaps imagining himself a new John Kennedy, he recommended a 200-mile naval blockade zone around the Falklands, and cited the precedent of the Cuban missile crisis. How apt. The Falklands should be repossessed and the SDP would support the Government in office to sustain this end, because servicemen's lives 'might be put at risk'. Tam Dalyell rose and asked

Owen to give way for a question. Owen refused, with an interesting response which shows that he knew he was silencing the voice of an opponent to the Task Force. 'There is no question of anyone in the House weakening the stance of the Government', Owen stated flatly. A wonderful thing, democracy. Dalyell rose again, but Owen ignored him and concluded, 'The House must now resolve to sustain the Government in restoring the position.' The Westminster SDP kept in with the mob.

Sir Julian Amery was then recognized by the Speaker, who so selected one of the more right-wing members of the House. For Amery, 'The third naval power in the world, and the second in NATO, has suffered a humiliating defeat.' With these opening words, he went on to attack the Foreign Office, particularly Lord Carrington, then the withdrawal from the naval base in Simonstown, South Africa, and next the run-down of the navy. He could not believe that the intelligence services had failed to detect the Argentine build-up. But:

> We have lost a battle, but have not lost the war. It is the old saying that Britain always wins the last battle. [Suez, for example?] 'I seek ... two simple assurances. The first is that we are determined to make the Argentine dictator disgorge what he has taken—by diplomacy if possible, by force if necessary ... nothing else will restore the credibility of the Government or wipeth stain from Britain's honour.

The Biblical archaism stiffened credibility all round. Britain will wipeth last.

A Labour voice was heard. He too had been involved in the 1977 action when his Government saved the Falklands. Furthermore, Ted Rowlands had a goddaughter in Port Stanley, who was there with her mother, in Argentinian hands. He had been involved with the islands 'over many years', and knew a lot about their people:

> If the honourable lady [Thatcher] meets the islanders, which I hope she will do—and I hope we shall succeed in freeing them—she will find that they are passionate believers in parliamentary democracy. They listen to and watch everything that we say and do in the House. It is one of their most remarkable characteristics. Even the most obscure parliamentary question is followed and debated in the Falkland Islands.

What with that and looking after 600,000 sheep, it's little wonder that most of them have remained laconic. But given how closely the Falklanders followed *Hansard*, how could the Government possibly have failed to follow the build-up of Argentinian intentions? Rowlands referred to his experience in office in 1977:

> We found out that certain attitudes and approaches were being

formed. I cannot believe that the quality of our intelligence has changed. Last night the Secretary of State for Defence asked, 'How can we read the mind of the enemy?' I shall make a disclosure. As well as trying to read the mind of the enemy, we have been reading its telegrams for many years.

Rowlands went on to relate how *he* had gone to Callaghan with information in 1977 and the then Prime Minister (and not David Owen?) had instructed the covert dispatch of a naval force. Now it was essential to restore the rights of the Falklanders 'as urgently as possible'. If the Government Ministers cannot do this, 'they should go'.

The islanders have already paid a high price for the initial set of blunders. They have lost their freedom for the first time in 150 years. The guilty men should not go scot free if we do not retrieve the islands as quickly as possible.

In Parliamentary terms, the pressure of this argument was very strong. It gave the Government no room for manoeuvre. 'We saved it, you have lost it, either you get it back or get out.' Had it been unemployment that was being debated, the rhetoric would be regarded as dull—run-of-the-mill verbiage that could be ignored if anyone bothered to listen. But it was the nation's honour that was at stake, in a contest in which each party seeks to represent the Nation, at the expense of the other.

Patrick Cormack followed, a representative of Tory sagacity at its deepest. Michael Foot was great, 'for once he truly spoke for Britain'. So too did Dr Owen. This should give 'fortification' to the Prime Minister.

But what a blunder, what a monumental folly, that the Falkland Islanders should be incarcerated in an Argentine goal .... It was not right that the Foreign Secretary should have been absent from the United Kingdom during this week .... These things must be said because we are talking about redeeming a situation. We are talking about restoring credibility. That is restoring the credibility not merely of a set of politicians and of a Government, *but of our nation*. We must all be determined to do that. [My emphasis.] ... This is one of the most critical moments in the history of our country since the war .... I should think that there will be some anxious people in Gibraltar today. (An Honourable Member: 'And in Hong Kong'.) There will also be anxious people in Hong Kong .... Therefore, our united resolve from today must be to utilize the unanimity that has been expressed in the debate.

Unless the Government did so *utilize* this unanimity Cormack warned, he would leave the Tory benches.

Arthur Bottomley was selected next from Labour. Would he finally staunch the flow of gibberish from the other side? No. He simply asked the Prime Minister a brief question: would she assure our friends 'that so long as the Falkland Islands and their inhabitants wish to remain in the Commonwealth, Britain will see that they do so?' Eh? It seems that Bottomley's national-internationalism had not yet caught up with the UN and that he still believes in the Commonwealth. It was its only mention as an institution. But then Bottomley was Colonial Secretary when the Smith Junta seized power in Rhodesia ....

Bottomley was followed by a Conservative, Raymond Whitney, who was interrupted six times in ten minutes by formal questions and was subjected throughout to an intense and furious barrage of heckling and disruption from his own side of the gangway. Whitney had worked in Argentina for the Foreign Office during the early seventies, and thus knew something about the matter. This was intolerable. 'The Foreign Office was not working for Britain', said the first interjector, Teddy Taylor. The sixth and last objected intensely to Whitney's suggestion that 'there are alternative ways in which the interests of the Falklands Islanders can be protected and I feel that these can be achieved by negotiation.' Sir John Biggs-Davison of Epping Forest was beside himself, and interrupted on a point of order: 'If defeatism of this kind is to be spoken, should it not be done in secret session? Would it be in order to spy strangers?' (Had the 'Honourable' member so 'spied', the Speaker would have had to ask visitors to leave the galleries.) Over the howls and caterwauls, Whitney retorted: 'it is not a question of defeatism—it is a question of realism and the avoidance of another humiliation for our country.'

This was the only point in the whole debate when the interests of the islanders as people were directly addressed. The reality was unbearable. For the House they were *symbols* of British pride; of the country's holy freedoms (to be unemployed, to love the Queen, but not to vote); of democracy; of sovereignty. Whitney pleaded with the collective wisdom of the Commons: could it not consider the consequences of war carefully? Would not the implications of a successful landing mean a military presence for years?

> I earnestly implore the House to think very carefully, so that we make sure that we are ready to take and answer the challenges of the questions that are there. They will not go away if they are not enunciated.

It was a brave but futile effort, like asking a cage of parrots to think before they speak.

The Foreign Affairs representative of the Liberal Party rose. Perhaps he, at least, would also bring some thought to the affair. He reprimanded Whitney, however, and told him: 'This is without doubt a very shameful day for this country.' In that he was correct, if not in the way he imagined. Russell Johnston (of Inverness) then quoted from an editorial in the *Guardian*, which stated, 'the Falkland Islands do not represent any strategic or commercial British interest worth fighting over (unless one believes reports of crude oil under its off-shore waters.)' It was an odd assertion, playing the issue on both sides of the street and thus failing to keep even to the middle of the road. Exactly how much oil would be 'worth' fighting for, and exactly how many dead would make it worthwhile, and to whom, are questions that could fill pages with evasive answers. Johnston was clever to upbraid it. It allowed him to score a cheap point and proclaim that it was the 'rights and freedoms of individual people' that mattered. He was 'depressed' and 'angry' to see photographs of Galtieri looking pleased. Johnston then told the House how he was a member of the Falkland Islands Association. He had followed the issue and knew that government after government had starved the place of funds. Now 'vast amounts of money will have to be spent'. 'If we are to act at all, we must act swiftly.'

Sir John Eden was then selected to address the House with his distinctive point of view. The Foreign Office, he thought, or at least 'elements' within it 'have been wanting to be rid of what they have regarded as a tiresome problem.' How dull and sensible. But now, revenge would be exacted, to preserve by force one of the few remaining colonies as Sir Nigel Fisher had described it. The species would not be allowed to become extinct while knights such as Sir Nigel and Sir John had any sway. Force must be mounted, said Sir John, the Government was committed, Thatcher should make sure that her commitment, 'is carried through to the earliest possible fulfilment. The honour of the country demands nothing less.'

Donald Stewart, a Scottish Nationalist from the Western Isles, was then recognized. He too had constituents who worked in the Falklands and he was also a member of the Falklands lobby. The sequence of Sir John Eden followed by Donald Stewart, as speakers in the 'debate', revealed one of its determining patterns. On the one hand a succession of ultra-right-wing Tories from the South Coast (Sir John Eden represents Bournemouth West); on the other, MPs from the Celtic fringe with Falkland interests. It would be hard to think of a less representative combination for the defence of British democracy. Argentina's claims to the sovereignty of the Falklands were 'totally unfounded' according to Stewart. The Government should have been prepared. 'I hope that this matter can be resolved without force, but if force is necessary, so be it.'

The MP for Honiton, Devonshire, came next. Sir Peter Emery regarded the House as 'absolutely unanimous', with 'perhaps one exception'.

> The British House of Commons is determined to ensure that the British Falkland Islands people shall be removed from the yoke of the Argentine Government .... We must risk nothing that could bring about defeat .... If that action of withdrawal has not been taken within 10 or 14 days stipulated by the Government, a state of war should exist between Argentina and Britain.

At last a pillar from the Labour Party rose, a man of experience with a constituency in a major city: Douglas Jay from London's Battersea. But it was possible to distinguish him from the previous speaker only by the degree of grammatical coherence and ordered phraseology that he brought to his demand for war.

> The Foreign Office is a bit too much saturated with the spirit of appeasement. I hope that, apart from anything else, the Foreign Office will now examine its conscience, if it has one. Second, I trust ... that there will be no cash limits on any effective action that we now take. Thirdly ... Diplomacy can succeed only if it is visibly supported by effective action .... What matters now is that these people wish to remain British, and that is the right to self-determination ... as the whole history of this century has shown, if one gives way to this sort of desperate, illegal action, things will not get better, they will get worse.

It is possible to discern a difference in mental attitude of the southern Tory knights from that of the squires of Labourism. The former are more intensely patriotic. It is the internal decay and shrivelling of what it means to be British, that upsets them. For the Labour nationalists, however, it is the decline of Britain in the world that matters; theirs is the more external, global and 'historical' perspective.

Up popped Sir Bernard Braine (Conservative) to prove the point. He began his remarks with an astute observation of the occasion: 'This remarkable debate has been characterised by high-calibre speeches showing acute perception of the problem.' And he went on to add his own finely engineered perceptions, concluding:

> The time for weasel words has ended. I expect action from the Government; and I hope that we shall get it. However, let there be no misunderstanding. Unless the Falkland Islands are quickly restored to lawful British sovereignty, and unless their people are freed from the dreadful shadow under which they have lived for a decade or more, the effect on the Government will be dire.

He had already stated that he would withdraw his support from the Government if it failed in its duty. In Parliamentary terms, this meant that Sir Bernard and his bunch of diehards would support an Opposition motion of censure on the Government for its handling of the Falklands, unless Thatcher and her Cabinet acted with full determination. Only 30 fanatics would be needed to march into the lobby behind Michael Foot and Douglas Jay to bring down the appeasers.

Sir Bernard's speech was not quite finely calculated enough, in the tactical sense. Had he gone on foaming a bit longer, his would have been the last contribution to the 'debate' before the two winding-up speeches from the front-benches. Nor was the full force of Sir Bernard's passion communicated by the tidy columns of *Hansard*.

> The very thought that our people, 1,800 people of British blood and bone, could be left in the hands of such criminals is enough to make any normal Englishman's blood—and the blood of Scotsmen and Welshmen—boil too.

It was so much finer to hear than to read. He was apoplectic: 'B B B British b b b blood and b b bone' he stammered. 'Any normal Englishman's b b blood', he raved on, in full flight, drugged by ethnicity, when some slight mental process stirred as he recalled that it was Britain, not England, he was supposed to speak for. The islanders are—to a *man* (women have yet to enter his consciousness as other than victims it seems)—mainly Scottish and Welsh. The English who are involved with the Falklands to any significant degree are its absentee landlords, shareholders in the Falkland Islands Company and Empire-minded MPs. So Sir Bernard quickly threw the blood of the Scotsman and the Welshman back into the boiling brew.

An outsider coming into the visitors' gallery of the House of Commons at that moment might have asked why the honourable member's blood was so disturbed. Was it because four million of his fellow citizens had been deprived of a paying job? Was it that good, higher education was being dismantled in the United Kingdom? Was it that a million of Sir Bernard's fellow Englishmen who happen to be black were being subjected to excessively firm police measures? Was it even due to the Falkland Islanders being deprived of their right of 'self-determination'? Of course not. It was none of these things. The visitor would simply have witnessed the froth and curdle of an old ruling class now going off its rocker.

Finally, a voice from Scotland was heard to demand some—a bit—of proportion. George Foulkes was recognized. We know why, as Tam Dalyell has explained, 'I went to the Speaker's Secretary, standing by his chair, to ask him to call a dissenting voice'.[18] The great 'debate' had been a pre-selected beauty contest with only those whose patriotic features were deemed bulbous enough, allowed to display themselves before the public. The Speaker gave way at the very end.. Foulkes had four minutes to 'dissent'. But he felt completely on the defensive:

I have some reservations about what seems to have been emerging, almost unanimously, as the view of the House.

He was interrupted, and replied:

My gut reaction is to use force. Our country has been humiliated. Every honourable member must have a gut reaction to use force. But we must also be sure that we shall not kill thousands of people in the use of that force ... I am against the military action for which so many people have asked because I dread the consequences that will befall the people of our country and the people of the Falkland Islands.

Gut reactions and the sentiment of dread were hardly a convincing way to argue an alternative.

The two concluding speeches followed, the first from John Silkin, Labour's shadow spokesman for defence. His was probably the most hypocritical of all the contributions. He began by claiming that Michael Foot was now 'the leader of the nation'. The day was not one for judgements or recriminations however—Silkin agreed. He then dedicated his entire speech to often skilful recriminations against the Government, and judged that the Prime Minister should go. She, the Secretary for Defence and the Secretary for Foreign Affairs, 'are on trial today'. Silkin's conclusion to them: 'The sooner you get out the better.'

Between scoring points against the Thatcher Government, Silkin assured the House that, 'Our thoughts are with our fellow citizens in the Falkland Islands' (his thoughts were thus not at all on gaining office for himself). With Parliament so steamed up, nobody would interject that the Falklanders were not in fact 'fellow citizens' but second-class subjects. Silkin had a more touching sentiment yet:

I make one appeal above all others to the Government. Let us ensure that our dear fellow citizens in the Falkland Islands are kept in touch with us as much as possible. Let us extend our broadcasts.

As for Galtieri, the worst in a bunch of fascists:

When he says to us that he will respect the rights and property and, above all, the lives and freedom of our people, we have a right to wonder whether this is true in view of what he does to his own people.

Oh, he said that, did he? It is strange that nobody mentioned the Junta's pledge during the debate, in which the Falklanders' 'rights' figured so prominently. Only Michael Foot had glimpsed the possible embarrassment of this aspect of the Argentine take-over, to dismiss it in advance. Fortunately, with the debate being so short and the speakers so 'representative', no MP who spoke was foolish enough to demand that the Junta's offer be seriously tested. Naturally, one would have to do much more than 'wonder' at the veracity of Galtieri's promise; yet measures could have been suggested to help ensure that such a promise was observed. To speak like this, however, would be to speak treason: to face realities and care for people rather than defending sovereignty. No such blackguard rose to shame the House from the opposition front-bench.

John Nott, Secretary of State for Defence, then made the final contribution to the day's discussion. He did not address himself seriously to the future. As he tried to defend the Government's lack of preparation almost all of Nott's speech concerned the past. How could it have allowed Argentina to have walked over the Falklands? Why had he not taken some preemptive action to deter the aggression, as Labour had in 1977? Wasn't it he who had run down the navy? Nott struggled with little conviction to defend the record. Goaded beyond endurance he asked the House:

> If we were unprepared, how is it that from next Monday, at only a few days notice, the Royal Navy will put to sea in wartime order and with wartime stocks and weapons? ... I suggest that no other country in the world could react so fast and the preparations have been in progress for several weeks.

Several weeks? An exceedingly interesting suggestion, especially as it came from the Secretary of State for Defence himself.

Nott then concluded. He told the House that the situation was 'extremely grave'.

> We intend to solve the problem and we shall try to solve it continuingly by diplomatic means, but if that fails, *and it will probably do so*, we shall have no choice but to press forward with our plans. (My emphasis.)

One of these 'plans' had already fallen into place:

> We can at least ... give to the armed forces the unanimous backing of the House in the difficult task that they are being asked to undertake.

The 'unanimous' House of Commons adjourned. Britain had been sent to war.

3   Churchillism

TO LISTEN to the House of Commons debate on 3 April 1982 was like tuning in to a Wagnerian opera. Counterpoint and fugue rolled into an all-enveloping cacophony of sound and emotion. Britannia emerged once more, fully armed and to hallelujahs of assent (accompanied by fearful warnings should She be again betrayed). A thunderous 'hear, hear' greeted every audacious demand for revenge wrapped thinly in the call for self-determination. Dissent was no more than a stifled cough during a crescendo of percussion: it simply confirmed the overwhelming force of the music.

Later, opposition would make itself heard above the storm. But it was drowned out at the crucial moment. In part this was arranged. As we have seen, scheming took place to ensure a 'united House'. MPs took six days to debate entry into the Common Market in 1973. They went to war for the Falklands in three hours. The result was to preempt public discussion with a fabricated consensus. In the immediate aftermath of Argentina's take-over of the islands, most people could hardly believe it was more important than a newspaper headline about some forgotten spot. Suddenly they were presented with the unanimous view of all the party leaders that this was a grave national crisis which imperilled Britain's profound interests and traditional values. The decisive unity of the Commons was thuggish as well as inspired. The few who feared the headlong rush were mostly daunted and chose the better part of valour. Innocent islanders in 'fascist' hands, the nation's sovereignty raped: it seemed better to wait and let things calm down. The war party seized the occasion with the complicity of the overwhelming majority of MPs from all corners of Parliament. On 3 April there was scarcely an opposition to be outmanoeuvred. The result was that even if one continued to regard the Falklands as insignificant, there clearly *was* a Great Crisis. Within what is called 'national opinion' there was no room to disagree about that: one had either to concur or suffocate. The Commons united placed British sovereign pride upon the line; and sovereignty is not a far away matter, people feel it here at home just as they identify with their national team in a World Cup competition, however distant. With a huge endorsement from the press, Parliament had ensured that the nation—so we were told—spoke with one voice, had acted with purpose and solidarity and had thus gambled its reputation on a first-class military hazard.

Many trends were at work—consciously or blindly—to prepare for such a moment. But much more important, and what gave the militants the 'unity' essential to their cause, was the general condition that allowed them to succeed so handsomely. It held the Commons in the palm of its hand. It orchestrated the one-nation sentiments of the three geniuses of the occasion—Enoch Powell, Michael Foot and David Owen—who bound Thatcher so willingly to *Hermes*. To analyse this general condition properly would take a thick book, for it has many symptoms. Moreover the condition is so deeply and pervasively a part of England, so natural to its political culture, that it is difficult to see, impossible to smell as something distinct. Like the oxygen in the air we breathe, and which allows flames to burn, it is ordinarily intangible. Perhaps the Falklands crisis will at last bring the mystery into sight.

To provoke and assist this discussion of the pathology of modern British politics, I will be bold and assertive. Yet it should be borne in mind that I am only suggesting a possible description; one which will certainly need correction and elaboration. First, we need a name for the condition as a whole, for the fever that inflames Parliamentary rhetoric, deliberation and decision. I will call this structure of feeling shared by the leaders of the nation's political life, 'Churchillism'. Churchill*ism* is like the warp of British political culture through which all the main tendencies weave their different colours. Although drawn from the symbol of the wartime persona, Churchillism is quite distinct from the man himself. Indeed, the real Churchill was reluctantly and uneasily conscripted to the compact of policies and parties which he seemed to embody. Yet the fact that the ideology is so much more than the emanation of the man is part of the secret of its power and durability.

Churchillism was born in May 1940, which was the formative moment for an entire generation in British politics. Its parliamentary expression was a two-day debate which ended on 8 May with a crucial division on the Government's conduct of the war. Churchill himself had already entered the cabinet, which remained under Chamberlain's direction. After the hiatus of the 'phony war', an attempt by the British to secure control of Norway had ended in disaster. Although Churchill also bore responsibility for the misadventure, it was Chamberlain who was felt to be out of step with the time. Attlee asked for different people at the helm. From the Conservative back-benches Leo Amery repeated a testy remark of Cromwell's, 'In the name of God, go!'. The Government's potential majority of 240 crashed to 80. In the aftermath Churchill emerged as Prime Minister with, as I will discuss in a moment, the crucial support of Labour to create a new National Coalition. Within days, the war took on a dramatically different form, and then a catastrophic one, as the Germans advanced across Holland and into France. The British army was encircled and the order to evacuate given on 27 May. Through good fortune some 300,000 were pulled back across the Channel and Dunkirk became a symbol not only of survival but also of 'national reconciliation' and ultimate resurgence as it coincided with the emergence of Churchill's coalition.[1]

At that moment Churchill himself was a splendid if desperate enemy of European fascism, while Churchill*ism* was the national unity and coalition politics of the time. Among those who participated most enthusiastically, there were some who wanted to save Britain in order to ensure the role of the Empire, and others who wanted to save Britain in order to create a new and better order at home. But Churchillism was more than a mere alliance of these attitudes. It incorporated imperialists and social democrats, liberals and reformers.[2] From the aristocrats of finance capital to the autodidacts of the trade unions, the war created a social and political amalgam which was not a fusion—each component retained its individuality—but which nonetheless transformed them all internally, inducing in each its own variety of Churchillism and making each feel essential for the whole.

Today Churchillism has degenerated into a chronic deformation, the sad history of contemporary Britain. It was Churchillism that dominated the House of Commons on 3 April 1982. All the essential symbols were there: an island people, the cruel seas, a British defeat, Anglo-Saxon democracy challenged by a dictator, and finally the quintessentially Churchillian posture—we were down but we were not out. The parliamentarians of right, left and centre looked through the mists of time to the Falklands and imagined themselves to be the Grand Old Man. They were, after all, his political children and they too would put the 'Great' back into Britain.

To see how the Falklands crisis brought the politicians at Westminster together and revealed their shared universe of Churchillism, it will help to note the separate strands which constituted it historically: Tory belligerents, Labour reformists, socialist anti-fascists, the liberal intelligentsia, an entente with the USA (which I will look at at greater length as its legacy is crucial) and a matey relationship with the media.

1.   Tory Imperialists

In 1939 only a minority of the Conservative Party supported Churchill in his opposition to appeasement. Their motives for doing so were mixed. The group included back-bench imperialists like Leo Amery—the father of Sir Julian Amery, who spoke in the Falklands debate—and 'one nation' reformers like the young Macmillan. A combination of overseas expansionism and social concessions had characterized Conservatism since Disraeli: a nationalism that displaced attention abroad plus an internal policy of gradualist, paternalistic reform.

Churchill, however, stood on the intransigent wing of the Party. (He had left the Conservative front bench over India in 1931 when he opposed granting it dominion status.) Unlike Baldwin, Churchill had ferociously resisted the rise of Labour, and his militancy in the General Strike made him an enemy of the trade unions until he finally took office in May 1940. Three years previously Baldwin had retired and been replaced by Chamberlain who was efficient but also aloof and stubborn. He proved incapable of assimilating Labour politicians into his confidence, while he saw the imperative need for peace if British business interests were to prosper. By continuing to exclude the restless Churchill from office, Chamberlain perhaps ensured that he would see the opposite and indeed, Churchill gave priority to military belligerency. Thus Churchill, who had initially welcomed Mussolini as an ally in the class war, became the most outspoken opponent of Nazism, because it was a threat to British power. There was no contradiction in this, but rather the consistency of a Toryism that in the last instance placed the Empire before the immediate interests of trade and industry.

2. Labour and Reformism

As emphasized earlier, it is essential that Churchill and Churchillism be rigorously distinguished. While the man had been among Labour's most notorious enemies, the 'ism' contains Labour sentiment as one of its two major pillars. In terms of Churchill's own career, the transformation can be seen in 1943, when he sought the continuation into the postwar period of the coalition government with Labour. Conversely, the Labour Party's support was crucial in Churchill's accession to power in May 1940. Chamberlain had actually maintained a technical majority in the vote over the failure of the Norwegian expedition; but the backlash was so great that his survival came to depend on Labour's willingness to join his government. It refused, asserting that it would only join a coalition 'as a full partner in a new government under a new Prime Minister which would command the confidence of the nation'. Within an hour of receiving this message, Chamberlain resigned.[3]

It is important to recall that Chamberlain's régime was itself a form of coalition government. At the height of the depression in 1931, Ramsey MacDonald had decapitated the Labour Movement by joining a predominantly Conservative alliance. This incorporation of part of the Labour leadership into a basically Tory government was a triumph for Baldwin, vindicating his strategy of deradicalizing the Labour movement through the cooptation of its parliamentary representatives. By the same token, the creation of the 1931 National Government was a defeat for the hardline approach of Churchill. The great irony of 1940, then, was that Labour attained its revenge by imposing the leadership of its former arch-enemy on the Tory Party. The alliance which resulted was also quite different from the National Government of 1931: that first coalition broke the Labour Party while in 1941 it was the Conservatives who were 'shipwrecked'.[4]

Churchill dominated grand strategy but Labour transformed the domestic landscape. Ernest Bevin, head of the Transport and General Workers Union, became Minister of Labour and a major figure in the War Cabinet. Employment rose swiftly as the economy was put on a total war footing and for the first, and so far only time in the history of British capitalism, a significant redistribution of wealth took place in favour of the disadvantaged. While adamant in his attitude towards strikes and obtaining a more complete war mobilization than in Germany, Bevin ensured the extension of unionism and improvements in factory conditions. Both physically massive men, the collaboration of Churchill and Bevin personified the contrast with the earlier pact between Baldwin and MacDonald. The 1931 National Government was a formation of the centre based on compromise at home and abroad. The two prime actors in 1941 were men of deeds, determined to pursue their chosen course. Once enemies, they now worked together: an imperialist and a trade unionist, each depending upon the other.

Within the alliance, the centre worked away. To compound the ironies involved, some of the Conservatives who most readily accepted the domestic reforms were from the appeasement wing of the party. Butler, for example, who disdained Churchill even after the war began, put his name to the 1944 Education Act that modernized British education (though it preserved the public school system). But the administrative reformists of the two main parties never captured the positions of ideological prominence. Bevin was more a trade union than a Parliamentary figure, Attlee led from behind, and Labour in particular suffered from its inability to transform its 'moral equality' into an equivalent ideological hegemony over the national war effort.

3. Anti-Fascism

Overarching the centre was an extraordinary alliance of left and right in the war against fascism. Those most outspoken on the left were deeply committed to the war effort (even when their leading advocate in the Commons, Aneurin Bevan, remained in opposition).

The patriotic anti-fascists of both Left and Right had different motives, but both had a *global* perspective which made destruction of Nazism their first imperative. When the Falklands war party congratulated Michael Foot—the moral anti-fascist without equal on the Labour benches—for his stand, it was like a risible spoof of that historic, formative moment in World War Two when the flanks overwhelmed the centre to determine the execution of the war.

Yet it was not a hoax, it was the real thing; though it related to 1940 as damp tea-leaves to a full mug. The Falklands debate was genuinely Churchillian, only the participants in their ardour failed to realize that they were the dregs. This is not said to denigrate either the revolutionaries or the imperialists of the World War. Their struggle against fascism was made a mockery of in Parliament on 3 April: for example, when Sir Julien Amery implicitly, and Douglas Jay explicitly, condemned the Foreign Office for its 'appeasement', just because it wanted a peaceful settlement with Buenos Aires; or when Patrick Cormack said from the Tory benches that Michael Foot truly 'spoke for Britain'.[5]

Above all, it was a histrionic moment for Foot. Although frequently denounced by the Right as a pacifist, he was in fact one of the original architects of bellicose Labour patriotism. Working on Beaverbrook's *Daily Express* he had exhorted the Labour movement to war against the Axis. In particular, in 1940 when he was 26, he inspired a pseudonymous denunciation of the appeasers called *The Guilty Men*, published by Gollancz. Foot demanded the expulsion of the Munichites—listed in the booklet's frontispiece—from the government, where Churchill had allowed them to remain. *The Guilty Men* instantly sold out and went through more than a dozen editions. It contains no socialist arguments at all, but instead is a dramatized accounting of the guilt of those who left Britain unprepared for war and the soldiers at Dunkirk unprotected. It points the finger at Baldwin and MacDonald for initiating the policy of betrayal. On its jacket it flags a quote from Churchill himself, 'The use of recriminating about the past is to enforce effective action at the present'. Thus while the booklet attacks both the Conservative leadership of the previous decade and the Labour men who sold out in 1931, it impeaches them all alike on patriotic grounds: they betrayed their country. Churchill's foresight and resolve, by contrast, qualify him for national leadership—for the sake of the war effort, the remaining 'guilty men' had to go.

It was precisely this rhetoric—the language of *Daily Express* socialism—that was pitched against the Thatcher government in the 3 April debate by the Labour front-bench. Foot denounced its leaders for failing to be prepared and for failing to protect British people against a threat from dictatorship. The 'Government must now prove by deeds ... that they are not responsible for the *betrayal* and cannot be faced with that *charge*. That is the charge, I believe, that lies against them.' (my emphasis) Winding up, John Silkin elaborated the same theme, only as he was concluding the debate for the opposition he was able to bring the 'prosecution' to its finale, in the full theatre of Parliament. Thatcher, Carrington and Nott 'are on trial today', as 'the three most guilty people'.

4. Liberalism
The political alliance of Churchillism extended much further than the relationship between Labour and Conservatives. The Liberals were also a key component, and this helps to explain why an important element of the English intelligentsia was predominantly, if painfully, silent at the outbreak of the Falklands crisis. In 1940 the Liberals played a more important role in the debate that brought down Chamberlain than did Labour spokesmen, with Lloyd George in particular making a devastating intervention. Later, individual Liberals provided the intellectual direction for the administrative transformation of the war and its aftermath.

Keynes was its economic architect, Beveridge the draughtsman of the plans for social security that were to ensure 'no return' to the 1930s. Liberalism produced the 'civilized' and 'fair-minded' critique of fascism, which made anti-fascism acceptable to Conservatives and attractive to aristocrats. Liberalism, with its grasp of detail and its ability to finesse issues of contention, was the guiding spirit of the new administrators. Because of its insignificant party presence, its wartime role is often overlooked, but liberalism with a small 'l' was the mortar of the Churchillian consensus. One of Beveridge's young assistants, a Liberal at the time, saw the way the wind was blowing and joined the Labour Party to win a seat in 1945. His name was Harold Wilson.[6]

5. The American Alliance and 'Self-Determination'
Churchillism was thus an alliance in depth between forces that were all active and influential. Nor was it limited to the domestic arena; one of its most important constituents has been its attachment to the Anglo-American alliance, and this was Churchill's own particular achievement. Between the wars the two great anglophone powers were still as much competitors as allies. During the 1920s their respective general staffs even reviewed war plans against one another, although they had been allies in the First World War. The tensions of the Anglo-American relationship four decades ago and more may seem irrelevant to a discussion of the Falklands affair; yet they made a decisive contribution to the ideological heritage which was rolled out to justify the dispatch of the Armada.

When Churchill took office in 1940 Britain was virtually isolated in Europe, where fascist domination stretched from Warsaw to Madrid, while the USSR had just signed a 'friendship' treaty with Germany and the United States was still neutral. Joseph Kennedy, the American ambassador in London (and father of the future President), was an old intimate of the Cliveden set and a non-interventionist. He had advised Secretary of State, Cordell Hull, that the English 'have not demonstrated one thing that could justify us in assuming any kind of partnership with them'.[7] But Roosevelt, eminently more pragmatic, saw that genuine neutrality would allow Hitler to win; it would lead to the creation of a massive pan-European empire, hegemonic in the Middle East and allied to Japan in the Pacific. On the other hand, by backing the weaker European country—the United Kingdom—the US could watch the tigers fight. Continental Europe would be weakened and Britain—especially its Middle East positions—would become dependent on Washington's good will. In other words, it was not fortuitous that America emerged as the world's greatest economic power in 1945, it simply took advantage of the opportunity that was offered. But this opportunity also provided Britain with its only possible chance of emerging amongst the victors. At issue were the *terms* of the alliance.

On May 15, immediately after he became Prime Minister and just before Dunkirk, Churchill wrote his first letter to Roosevelt in his new capacity. He asked for fifty old American destroyers and tried to lure the President away from neutrality. The Americans in turn suggested a swap arrangement that would give them military bases in the Caribbean, Newfoundland and Guyana. The trade of bases for old hulks was hardly an equal exchange, but by deepening American involvement it achieved Churchill's overriding purpose, and allowed the President to sell his policy to Congress. Later, as Britain ran out of foreign reserves, Lend-Lease was conceived. The United States produced the material of war while the British fought, and in the meantime relinquished their once commanding economic position in Latin America to Uncle Sam.[8] (So when Peron—whose country had been a British dominion in all but name for half a century—challenged the hegemony of the Anglo-Saxon bankers in 1946 by resurrecting the irredentist question of the Malvinas, it was a demagogic symbol of already fading subordination that he singled out. The real economic power along the Plata now resided in Wall Street rather than the City.)

Four months before Pearl Harbor, the 'Atlantic Charter' (August 1941) consolidated the Anglo-American alliance and prepared US opinion for entry into war. The Prime Minister and the President met off Newfoundland and agreed to publicize a joint declaration. The main argument between them was over its fourth clause.

Roosevelt wanted to assert as a principle that economic relations should be developed 'without discrimination and on equal terms'. This was aimed against the system of 'imperial preferences' which acted as a protectionist barrier around the British Empire. Churchill moderated the American position by inserting a qualifying phrase before the clause. Behind the fine words of the Atlantic Charter there was a skirmish and test of wills between the two imperialisms. Although we can now see that the Charter was determined by self-interest, its function was to enunciate democratic principles that would ensure popular and special-interest support in both countries for a joint Anglo-Saxon war. Both governments announced that they sought no territorial aggrandizement or revision that did 'not accord with the freely expressed wishes of the peoples concerned'. Churchill later *denied* that this in any way related to the British colonies. He was to declare in 1942 that he had not become Prime Minister to oversee the liquidation of the British Empire. Nonetheless he also claimed to have drafted the phrase in the Charter which states that the UK and the US would 'respect the right of all people to choose the form of government under which they will live'.[9] There is a direct lineage between this declaration and Parliament's reaction to the Falklands.

By the end of the year America had entered the war as a full belligerent. On New Years Day 1942, twenty-six allied countries signed a joint declaration drafted in Washington which pledged support to the principles of the Atlantic Charter. Henceforward the alliance called itself the 'United Nations', and three years later a world organization of that name assembled for the first time. In its turn it enshrined the principles of 'self-determination' codified by Roosevelt and Churchill.

In his memoirs Churchill is quite shameless about the greatness of the empires, British and American, that collaborated together against the 'Hun'. But he cannot hide the constant tussle for supremacy that took place between them, within their 'Anglo-Saxon' culture, in which each measured its own qualities against the other. From their alliance, forced on the British by extreme adversity, came their declaration of democratic aims. Its objective was to secure support from a suspicious Congress that saw no profit in bankrolling an Empire which was a traditional opponent, and which was detested by millions of Irish and German-American voters. It had, therefore, to be assuaged with the democratic credentials of the emerging trans-Atlantic compact. Thus, in order to preserve the Empire within an alliance of 'the English speaking nations', Churchill—imperialist in bone and marrow—composed a declaration of the rights of nations to determine their own form of government.

In international terms, this ambiguity is the nodal point of Churchillism. By tracing, however sketchily, its outline, we can begin to decode the extraordinary scenes in the House of Commons on 3 April this year. Above all, it clarifies the ease with which those like Thatcher utilized the resources of the language of 'self-determination'. When she and Foot invoked the UN Charter to justify the 'liberation' of the Falklands because its inhabitants desire government by the Crown, they reproduced the sophistry of the Atlantic Charter. What particular resonance can such terms have for the British Right, when in other much more important circumstances like Zimbabwe they are regarded as the thin wedge of Communist penetration? The answer is to be found in Churchillism, which defended and preserved 'Great' Britain and its imperial order by retreating slowly, backwards, never once taking flight, while it elevated *aspirations for freedom* into a smoke-screen to cover its manoeuvre.

In 1940 what was at stake was Britain's *own* self-determination. Invasion was imminent and an embattled leadership had to draw upon more than national resources to ensure even survival. Together with the invocation of specifically British values and tradition, Churchill revived the Wilsonian imagery of 'the great democratic crusade' (a rhetoric that had been improvised in 1917, in response to the Russian Revolution). Such ideals were crucial not only for the North American public but also for anti-fascist militants in the UK and for liberals, who loathed warfare—the experience of 1914–18 was still fresh—and who distrusted Churchill, especially for his evident pleasure in conflict. They were uplifted by the rallying cry that gave both a moral and political purpose to the war as it coupled the UK to its greatest possible ally. While Churchill saved Great Britain, preserved its institutions and brought its long colonial history to bear through his personification of its military strengths, he did so with a language that in fact opened the way for the Empire's dissolution. The peculiarity of this explains how Britain could shed—if often reluctantly and with numerous military actions—so many peoples and territories from its power after 1945 without undergoing an immediate convulsion, or any sort of outspoken political crisis commensurate with its collapse. Instead a long drawn-out anaemia and an extraordinary collective self-deception was set in train by Churchillism.

Perhaps the Falklands crisis will come to be seen as a final spasm to this process of *masked* decline. Many have seen it as a knee-jerk colonialist reaction. Foreigners especially interpret the expedition to 'liberate the Kelpers' as a parody of Palmerstonian gunboat diplomacy, out of place in the modern world. It may be out of place, but in British terms its impetus is modern rather than Victorian.

The stubborn, militaristic determination evinced by the Thatcher government, her instant creation of a 'War Cabinet' that met daily, was a simulacrum of Churchilliana. So too was the language Britain had used to defend its actions. Both rhetoric and policy were rooted in the formative moment of contemporary Britain, the time when its politics were reconstituted to preserve the country as it 'stood alone' in May 1940.[10] A majority of the population are today too young to remember the event, but most members of Parliament do. The mythical spirit of that anxious hour lives on as a well-spring in England's political psyche.

6. Incorporation of the Mass Media

There is one final aspect of Churchillism that needs to be mentioned: the relationship he forged with the media. He brought Beaverbrook into the Cabinet, attracted by the energy of the Canadian newspaper proprietor. He himself wrote in the popular press and took great care of his relations with the newspapers, in sharp contrast to Chamberlain who disdained such matters. Then, from 1940 onwards, Churchill's broadcasts rallied the nation: he skilfully crafted together images of individual heroism with the demand for general sacrifice. No subsequent politician in Britain has been able to forge such a bond between leader and populace.

The policies of the modern State are literally 'mediated' to the public via the political and geographical centralization of the national press. London dominates through its disproportionate size, its financial strength and the spider-web of rail and road of which it is the centre. Its daily press has long provided the morning papers for almost all of England, and they are taken by many in Scotland and Wales. A journalistic strike force has been developed, which strangely illuminates the way British political life is exposed to extra-national factors through its peculiar inheritance of capitalist aristocrats and overseas finance. Astor, an American, bought *The Times* in 1922; Thompson, a Canadian, acquired it in 1966; Rupert Murdoch, an Australian, took it over in 1981. But Astor, educated at Oxford, became anglicized and conserved the paper's character. The hegemonic organ of the nation may have been in the hands of a foreigner financially, but it was edited by Old England all the more because of it. Thompson pretended only to business rather than political influence, but he too made the transition across the Atlantic to become a Lord.

Thompson's son, however, shifted himself and the company back to North America, allowing a Catholic monetarist to lead the paper into the abyss of British labour relations and a year-long, futile closure. Now losing money heavily, *The Times* was sold to Murdoch, who already controlled the *News of the World* and the *Sun*. But he sojourns in New York rather than London. His papers endorsed the Falklands expedition with such a ludicrous enthusiasm that they managed to blemish vulgarity itself. But there remains a sense in which the relationship Churchill established with Beaverbrook came to be faintly echoed in Thatcher's reliance on Murdoch. The bombastic irrelevance of 'down under' helped Thatcher to storm the enfeebled ranks of gentry Conservatism, and gave her a major working-class daily—the *Sun*. Yet the *Sun*'s very lack of seriousness was a signal that the militarism of the Falklands War was bursting out of the carapace of Churchillism. The cardinal world issues adjudicated by Britain in the past could hardly be applied to taking on Argentina over 1,800 people in 1982. 'UP YOUR JUNTA', was one headline in the paper as it welcomed an initial British success. Was this the way to fight the scourge of fascism?

In 1940 Churchill was willing to do anything and everything for victory. Yet, as we have seen, the meaning of 'victory' became increasingly ambiguous in the course of the war. Churchill fought tooth and nail to defend the Empire, but in the end—to save British sovereignty itself—he formed, and was a prisoner of, a politics which accepted the liquidation of the Empire (except for a few residual outposts like the Falklands ...). The 'regeneration' was sufficiently radical to concede decolonialization and the emergence of new states, yet it was not radical enough to adapt the British State itself to its reduced stature. This, indeed, was its fatal success. Galvanized by total war, but, unlike continental Europe, spared the ultimate traumas of occupation and defeat, Britain survived the 1940s with its edifice intact. This fact has often been alluded to as a principal cause of the 'British disease'—the country's baffling postwar economic decline; moreover, it distinguished Churchillism from Gaullism.

The contrast is illuminating. Gaullism was born of defeat at the same moment as Churchillism (May 1940), and was also personified by a right-wing militaristic figure of equivalent self-regard and confidence. But in the long run Gaullism has inspired a far more successful national 'renewal' and adaptation to the increasingly competitive environment. Was this not partially due to the paradoxical fact that the fall of France, by reducing the Third Republic to rubble, ultimately provided a convenient building site for institutional modernization? In Britain, by contrast, the institutions held firm—like St Paul's defying the blitz—with corresponding penalties for this very durability. The most ingenious of Britain's defences against destructive change and forced modernization was the conserving collaboration between labour and capital. The relationship was the very core of Churchillism.

If Churchillism was born in May 1940, it had at least a twenty-year gestation. Keith Middlemas has shown that state, capital and labour sought to harmonize relations in a protean, tripartite affair after the crisis of the First World War. In his view, 'crisis-avoidance' became the priority after 1916 and has dominated British politics ever since. A significant degree of collaboration was achieved between the wars, often covertly, sometimes called 'Mondism' (after the man who headed the cartel that became ICI). One of the key figures on the Labour side was Citrine who led the TUC; another was Bevin, whose direction of manpower was, as we have seen, the backbone of Labour's contribution to Churchillism. Thus wartime corporatism radically intensified and made explicit an already established relationship. In Middlemas's words, 1940 instituted a 'political contract' where previously there had been an unwritten economic one.[11]

It is not my purpose here to try and add further to the list of elements involved. In academic terms it can be said—and it is important to say—that the picture is incomplete. Yet even when the skeleton is fully delineated we might still miss the unifying tissues. For Churchill*ism* was essentially the political flesh of national life: its skin, muscle tonality and arthritis. Churchillism *combined* the contradictions of capital and the workforce, as well as the desires for political freedom with those of imperial grandeur. Furthermore, it wedded these two distinct sets of opposites into a single enveloping universe of demagogy.

To help show that 'Churchillism' was not a momentary thing, born complete and fully armed from the jaws of defeat in 1940, but was itself a historical process we can glance at the events of late 1942. Churchill's role was contested to some degree from both left and right after May 1940, in the House of Commons and outside, especially as military defeats continued. It was only in November 1942 that the protests against his leadership ebbed away. That month was in fact the turning point of the war in Europe. It saw the Red Army turn the scales at Stalingrad and begin the destruction of Hitler's forces. It was also the month that the Americans landed in North Africa. This opened a small 'second front' as far away as possible from the main theatre, and signalled the arrival of the United States from across the Atlantic. The huge pincer movement that was to divide Europe between Moscow and Washington was underway, and it meant 'victory' for Britain as well.

Coincidentally, the Beveridge Report was published to massive acclaim at home. It held out the promise of full employment, a health service, adequate pensions and social benefits, at the end of the war. Not only was victory forthcoming, however hard the battles ahead, but the peace would be worth fighting for. Within two weeks of its publication in December 1942, a Gallup survey in the UK discovered that 19 out of 20 had heard of the Report and that 9 out of 10 thought that it should be accepted.[12]

Yet it was none of these things that ensured the supremacy of Churchill. The combination of American power and Beveridge could reassure the liberals, the coincidence of Stalingrad and the Report seemed to confirm hopes on the left. But what mattered most, pathetically so, was the victory at El Alamein. Finally, after months of bungling and defeats in Egypt and Libya, a huge concerted effort by the Empire swung the battle against Rommel, who was massively outgunned. In comparison with the Russian front, the adventures in the North African desert were a small sideshow (even then the British had at one point begun to evacuate Cairo). Yet for Churchill it was El Alamein that was the 'Hinge of Fate'. 'Before Alamein we never had a victory. After Alamein we never had a defeat', he suggested as his conclusion to the campaign.[13] In so far as 'we' meant the Allies, it was not only wrong (Midway had given the Americans control over the Pacific six months before); it was also fortuitous, as it preceded the far greater Russian breakthrough at Stalingrad by only a fortnight. But of course, the 'we' also meant the British, as if the entire course of the conflagration had been determined by the UK and its Empire. As the war was being won, it seemed that Churchill's Britain was winning the war; El Alamein secured his position at home politically. The battle also received disproportionate coverage in the UK, and has continued to do so across four decades of war books. The number of pages dedicated to North Africa has been an index of the desert war's ideological role in preserving British face, not its actual contribution to the world conflict. In this respect the current Falklands fanfare is its descendent.

The contrast in the aspirations represented by the conjuncture of El Alamein and the Beveridge Report was never reconciled by Churchill. His passion for Grand Imperial Strategy blinded him to the upsurge of hope amongst millions of his fellow countrymen, who longed simply for health and security. He took 'strong exception' to the Report and refused to commit the Coalition to its implementation after the war, pointing out that the financial demands it might make could conflict with the costs of occupying enemy countries.[14] When a Commons' debate on the Report was finally held, the Cabinet's prevarication and crassness left it remarkably isolated. All Labour members (bar one) who were not actually in government jobs voted against the Coalition's social paralysis. This firmly associated the Labour Party with the prospects for a new future; one historian considers that its Commons' vote then was probably responsible for winning the 1945 election.[15] The debate over Beveridge also led to the formation of a

Tory Reform Group that sought to reconcile the Conservatives to social change.

Which brings us to the *party* aspect of Churchillism and its legacy: the alternating two-party system, once heralded as proof of Britain's attachment to democracy and now under attack from the SDP as the cause of its decline. Not without reason, for each blames the other for the cocoon the two spun together after 1940. The reformers gained the ascendancy within the Conservative Party as Churchill remained aloof. The result was that despite his dominating national role, it was really Baldwin who was 'the architect of mid-century Conservatism' in attitude and spirit.[16] Yet Churchill's presence as leader of the opposition until 1951, and as Prime Minister again until 1955, prevented the overt expression of reformed Toryism from obtaining a positive, modern profile.

After his disastrous handling of the Beveridge Report, Churchill sensed the public swing away from him. In March 1943 he broadcast his own partial conversion to its principles and proposed a national coalition to continue into the postwar period. The Labour Party was unable to tolerate permanent institutionalization into a subordinate place, at least in such a naked form; it smacked too much of 1931. Rank-and-file militancy stiffened the resolve of the leaders to fight an election after the war. This opened the way for those merely sensible measures of nationalization undertaken by Labour after 1945 to be assailed as the most dreadful socialism by the Tory press. It has long been recognized that Labour's formative moment was not so much 1945 as 1940—Attlee was continuously in the Cabinet (first as Deputy Premier, then as Prime Minister) for over a decade. Labour, rather than the Tories, *built* the postwar consensus which was then *utilized* by the Conservatives.[17] To preserve this creative tension, with its invariable centrist bias, violent parliamentary attack was modulated with bipartisan understanding: Churchillism intensified and legitimized the operatics of pseudo-debate. And this was the price for so panoramic an incorporation.

Labour also inherited the full costs of Churchillism internationally. No sooner had Germany been defeated than the United States summarily severed Lend-Lease, making the abolition of the imperial preference system the precondition of any further financial aid. 'The American Loan' became the terrain of a major domestic and international battle over the financial and monetary autonomy of Labour reformism. With the installation of the coalition in May 1940, the old omnipotence of the Treasury over the national economy had been temporarily eclipsed—'in total war it was essential to plan resources first, leaving the financial side to be adjusted accordingly.'[18] In 1945 stringent American conditions helped clear the path for the restoration of the Treasury's authority. Moreover, the immediate financial crisis in war-exhausted Britain—fueled by the continuing foreign exchange shortage and gigantic debts to the dominions—was exacerbated by commitments to a high rate of military expenditure. One year later, for example, Britain still retained a garrison of 100,000 troops in both Egypt and Palestine. Despite Attlee's flirtation with a withdrawal from the Middle East, Bevin and the Chiefs of Staff persuaded him otherwise.[19] Soon the relative costs of Britain's military budget would become a major factor in the slippage of its economic power. Internalizing the Churchillian delusion of the country's destiny in the 'Grand Scheme', the Attlee government and subsequent Labour governments paid on the instalment plan the double costs of Churchillism: economic subordination to America and the projection of an independent world military role.

To sum up: Churchillism condemned to a slow death that which it saved from catastrophe. Its impulse was to preserve the Empire but Churchill was pragmatic enough to pay the costs of commitment to democracy—to 'self-determination' abroad and social reforms at home—that were anathema to the bedrock of his views. His militancy against Nazism made him welcome to the left, and Labour was crucial in putting him into office: it sustained the war effort that he spoke for. Thus Churchillism opened the way for the Labour victory in 1945, the creation of the welfare state, the legislated independence of India, and American domination. So too British socialism made its compromise with the capitalist nation under the benediction of Churchill's cigar and 'V' sign, which in turn crippled the modernizing, radical impulse of the social democrats and liberals who provided the brain power of the Labour Party in office. At the same time, Labour's international independence was clipped by the Cold War, itself dramatically announced by Churchill's famous 'Iron Curtain' speech of March 1946, where, in front of Truman, he called for Anglo-American military co-operation to be formalized into an anti-Soviet alliance.

At this point it may be pertinent to return to the analogy with Gaullism. Churchillism, as I have tried to show, is not a coherent ideology. Rather, it is an ideological matrix within which contending classes are caught, none of them being the 'true' exemplar since each is in some way equally constitutive. (Michael Foot was probably flabbergasted and bitter when Margaret Thatcher donned Churchill's mantle.) Gaullism, on the other hand, developed as an ideologically specific class force. It combatted Communist domination of the resistance movement and was not structurally penetrated by, or indebted to, the organized working class. This allowed the Gaullists a far greater confidence in their exercise of state power. *Dirigisme* and extensive nationalization were essential for the modernization of French capital, and under Gaullist colours the national could comfortably dominate over the social. In contrast, the legacy of Churchillism has been twofold: not only did it prevent the emergence of a nationally hegemonic Brandt/Schmidt type of social democracy, but it also blocked the Right from creating a dynamic party of national capital.

Andrew Gamble has distinguished three main schools of explanation for Britain's decline since 1945, and notes that there are Marxist as well as bourgeois variants of each. Respectively, these are: (1) the UK's over-extended international involvement and military expenditure; (2) archaic institutions of government including the party system; (3) the 'overloading' of the state by welfare expenditures, compounded by the entrenched position of the unions.[20] Each is partially true, but instead of arguing about which is the root cause of decline, we can note here that Churchillism fathered them all. Churchillism ensured that all parties were committed to a British military and financial role that was spun world wide; it conserved the Westminster system when it should have been transformed; it brought the unions into the system and initiated a welfare-state never efficiently dominated by social democracy. In short, Churchillism ensured the preservation of the Parliamentary Nation and thus Westminster's allegiance to a moment of *world* greatness that was actually the moment when the greatness ceased. Churchill's National Coalition ensured an astonishing recuperation, one that left the patient structurally disabled for the future and obsessed with magical resurrection from the dead.

4   Thatcherism

ON 3 JULY 1982, the Prime Minister spoke to her first major rally in the aftermath of the Falklands battle. Some 5,000 Conservative supporters gathered at Cheltenham racecourse, and Thatcher delivered one of the most remarkable speeches in recent British politics. She gave her interpretation of the True Meaning of the war in the South Atlantic. She announced that its 'spirit' would now be applied at home. The example of the task force was its professional leadership and its clear hierarchy of rank. 'Every man had his own task.' 'All were equally valuable—each was differently qualified.' This was a lesson not only for management—who should emulate the 'commanders in the field'—but also for the train drivers (then on strike) and the hospital ancillary workers engaged in industrial action. A lean, union-free, 'professional' economy led with martial élan was Margaret Thatcher's vision. For her it was more than a vision, the reality of it was already tangible.

Once, she said, there were some 'who thought that we could no longer do the great things which we once did'. Perhaps there were even some in that very Tory audience who had had 'secret fears ... that Britain was no longer the nation that had built an Empire and ruled a quarter of the world. Well they were wrong. The lesson of the Falklands is that Britain has not changed.' Other people might have thought that this was precisely the problem: that the UK had not changed while the rest of the world had. The fainthearts! No, a veritable renaissance was under way: 'We have to see that the spirit of the South Atlantic—the real spirit of Britain—is kindled not only by war but can now be fired by peace ... the spirit has stirred and the nation has begun to assert itself.' (See p. 149.)

Some days later, the polls registered Conservative party support running at close to 50% of the electorate with the rest divided between Labour and the Social Democrats, figures which promised Thatcher future re-election.

Thatcher's South Atlantic programme may appear implausible. But the less such aspirations are taken seriously, the more likely they are to succeed. Thatcher's prospectus capped a significant expression of opinion that began during the war itself and which has emerged from it strengthened as well as self-confident. As early as 14 May, *The Times*, as we will see, thought the war had awoken the

British people from their lethargy. On 5 April it had asserted that, 'the national will to defend itself has to be cherished and replenished'. A month later, satisfied that the 'will' had stirred, the paper insisted that it had to be fed with victory. Speaking to the annual conference of the Scottish Conservatives at Perth, a week before the British landings, Thatcher herself felt 'this ancient country rising as one nation .... Too long submerged, too often denigrated, too easily forgotten, the springs of pride in Britain flow again.' Sir Julian Amery had helped to set the tone with his intervention in the House of Commons debate on 20 May, the day before the British landing at San Carlos bay.

> What is at stake in the Falkland Islands crisis transcends the immediate issues of the Falkland Islanders and our own stake in the South Atlantic. The crisis is a catalyst of the basic values of our society; what Henry Kissinger has referred to as 'honour, justice and patriotism'. ... What is happening is not jingoism or war hysteria. It is the expression of a proud and ancient nation and of the most mature democracy in the world.

What more needs be said? Kissinger, the man who cabled Nixon to 'Bomb, bomb, bomb', is a perfect source for the ethics of Great Britain's moral re-armament, one which needs a real war to make it all the more complete. Until now chiliastic imperialists like Amery were not taken seriously, except as a gurgle of discontent on the back-benches of Westminster. Even the left used to look upon them with a kind of benevolence, as it seemed amusing to have a few of the old monsters around just as a reminder. Today, Amery's views must be listened to with a different sort of attention: he himself may remain as marginal as ever, but his attitudes are remarkably close to the ruling spirit of Thatcherite government. After the San Carlos bridgehead had been established, the *Economist* (29 May) took up the same theme:

> If the cooly professional British forces now on East Falklands bring the Argentine forces in Port Darwin and Port Stanley to an early recognition that they are beaten, there will be a surge of self-confidence within the British nation which could have great and lasting effects.

Leaving aside the multi-national complexity of the UK, what kind of nation is it that should need such a shot in the arm? Why should pushing a bullied, conscript army under the command of a notorious killer, from terrain few have desired to inhabit, be the source of 'great and lasting benefit'? Who could wish for a 'great surge' from such an unnecessary event?

There is both a recognition and a blindness to the somewhat fervid desires of *The Times* and the *Economist*, of Amery and

Thatcher. They are justified in feeling that something is wantonly wrong in the UK. The country's economic achievement is well below its potential. But they are blind to the impediments that have created and reinforced the blockage. How could it be otherwise when they are themselves spokesmen and women of one aspect of the impediment itself? They can hardly be expected to admit that they are themselves part of the problem rather than the country's saviours. Of course, I am over-simplifying. It is not the individuals themselves who are responsible, even collectively in the House of Commons, so much as an inherited, preserved and still energetic, institutional culture and economic orientation; one that impinges well beyond the political centre to the role of finance capital, the structure of industry, overseas investment and the labour movement.

It is difficult to explain this exactly without a full account of contemporary Britain. Despite the present recession and record unemployment, by no means everything has gone from bad to worse since 1945—there have been marked cultural and economic improvements. But the place of the British state in world affairs has rapidly diminished, just as its relative standard of living has fallen well behind its European neighbours. To take just one example of the UK's global position: at the beginning of the century, Britain produced a third of the world's exports of manufactures. Towards the end of the 1930s, this had fallen to nearly a fifth but rose again after the war to reach 25% by 1950. In the 1970s, however, the figure fell below 10% with no prospect of recuperation. One might argue that for a country of 50 million to have 9% of the world's exports in manufactures is more than adequate. But to a political class unable to accept such a status, the decline of Britain's world position is a blow to its 'natural' sovereignty (defined as it has to be in global terms). This apprehensive class seeks a way of 'pulling' the country out of its decline without abandoning its own world pretensions. This is the sublimated attraction of the Dunkirk spirit... (a favourite of Harold Wilson's). A turnaround is sought in which all 'pull together', and the institutions are preserved.

The idea that there was nothing *serious* holding the country back was captured in Wilson's election slogan of 1964: 'Let's Go With Labour'—now beyond irony. But his modernism turned out to be a veil which hid from sight his attachment to the old. Wilsonism foretold a 'technological revolution'. The unmasked archaicism of much of British life made his costume seem especially attractive. Yet by emphasizing the fripperies of history, Wilson ensured that he could leave untouched the central institutions of a retrograde order. In particular, he sacrificed Labour's social programmes to ensure that Britain met its financial 'obligations' overseas.[1] He refused to devalue the pound and condemned his administration to years of exchange crises. So Wilson turned to trade-union legislation for political salvation. But he was unable to ensure Labour Party backing and had to abandon his proposals, revealingly entitled 'In Place of Strife'. The episode contributed to his electoral defeat in 1970 and, with a strong supporting media chorus, helped to ensure the *fetishization* of the issue. Undoubtedly, embattled labour relations are a contributory factor to the UK's economic demise, even if they originated in the first place from its backward capitalism. But, however important, they are not the root problem taken on their own. They were projected into a central symbol of the British crisis in the 1960s and 1970s with an intensity that spoke of displacement, and this fixation on the unions diverted attention from equally critical problems, thereby contributing further to the general malaise.

When Heath replaced Wilson in 1970, his Government passed anti-union legislation and at the same time took Britain into the Common Market. Once more a 'magical' solution outside of the sovereign institutions themselves was conjured up to do the work of domestic transformation. Heath supposed that industry would be redirected and invigorated by its European context, while being liberated from the shackles of trade-union power.[2] Instead he was driven from office in a shambles of domestic conflict brought to a head by the second miners' strike. The fundamental reason for Heath's defeat in February 1974 was that he had launched perhaps the most far-reaching assault on the Churchillist inheritance, without adequately explaining what he was doing (indeed, there may be no rhetoric currently available in British politics to articulate such a programme). At any rate, when he announced in 1970 'we were returned to office to change the course of the history of this nation—nothing less',[3] Heath was hardly greeted with acclaim.

In the closing days of the February 1974 election, which Heath called to defeat the second national miners' strike, his campaign was hit by three blows: first, Enoch Powell, though saying he would die a Tory, announced that he would vote Labour and called on others to do likewise, because at least the Labour Party promised a referendum on the EEC and thus the possibility of a British withdrawal from it. Second, the head of the Confederation of British Industry said that the Industrial Relations Act should be repealed—the capitalists themselves disliked Heath's rigid labour legislation. Meanwhile a record trade deficit of nearly £400 million for January 1973 helped to undermine the credibility of Heath's economic transformation, made particularly painful by the year's 20% increase in food prices.[4] Heath's failure was a decisive event and it opened the way to Thatcher as well as to the

Wilson/Callaghan governments which her's would replace. Each government since Heath has sought retrogressive solutions to a crisis which had been greatly exacerbated by Heath's domestic fiasco.

In contrast to Heath's 'abrasiveness', Wilson now openly presented himself as a social conservative. He repealed the labour legislation and introduced a *Social Contract*. This was an attempt to codify publicly the relationship between the state and the labour movement, so crucial to Churchillism. But his attempt to make the understanding explicit was the harbinger of its destruction. Deftly retiring from office, Wilson was succeeded by Callaghan who was obliged to accept a conditional IMF loan while monetarist policies were introduced by his Chancellor, Denis Healey. If Wilson's answer to the crisis was to blame the Tories for being disruptive and to reassert the neo-corporatist formula of 1940, Callaghan tried to finessse the debacle of the *Social Contract* by following the example of Macmillan after Suez. He manoeuvred with flair and presented the image of a man for whom nothing was really out of sorts. The problem with such a pose, of course, is that it needs a fawning media to appear convincing. Callaghan did not have this, and when significant numbers of the working class voted for Thatcher in 1979, they did so because they knew that *something* was wrong.

So too did Margaret Thatcher and she campaigned on the need for measures to be taken. She offered 'change'. She saw the expanded role of the state and the 'relentless pursuit of equality' as the explanation of the British sickness, and promised an assault upon the 'progressive consensus' of the 1945 welfare state.[5] But while she has tried to cut back the role of the state in civil society (while increasing military expenditure), Thatcher nonetheless also considers it an essential part of her task that she should govern. 'Govern what?', one might ask, and the answer is to govern *firmly*. While Thatcher concurs that something is wrong, it is not the archaic nature of British sovereignty or the country's institutional traditions that she regards as being in need of transformation. Rather, she believes that they are not being exercised enough. Thatcher does not comprehend that Parliamentary rule needs to be reconstructed democratically, she thinks that it only needs to be *applied* with resolution and consistency for all to be well. In her view, what is missing is a lack of nerve and moral fibre. Thus she has, ironically, got closer to grasping that there is something wrong in 'the way' that Britain is governed, than those who simply blamed the unions, isolation from Europe, the role of sterling, etc. But Thatcher's solution—her gimmick—is that what is needed is 'real' British government. Her wing of the Tory party desires what it regards as a 'return' to home-made leadership that bears the once formidable impress of quality, 'Made in Britain'.

Such an approach ensured that a great deal less was actually made in Britain. 1980 saw the greatest-ever one year decline in British output.[6] Deindustrialization, a massive increase in unemployment, a surge in the export of capital, the regressive reform of taxation and decrease in real wage incomes—these might all have some rationality in terms of the peculiar structure of British capitalism, one dominated by the City and multinationals. But the combination was hardly designed to ensure electoral popularity. Hence the miraculous advent of the Falklands for Thatcher.

During the South Atlantic crisis, another issue more plausibly vital to British sovereignty cast an ironic light on the ensuing military battle. It illuminated the way the Falklands served to divert attention from the realities of the British economy—a diversion Thatcher positively welcomed when she spoke at Perth. One of the conventions of the EEC's procedures which had reassured the British on entry in 1973 was the so-called Luxembourg compromise. This was understood to be a crucial safeguard which meant that no member state could have its vital interests over-ruled by a majority vote of the others. Thatcher's government used the Luxembourg procedure as an instrument with which to veto Common Market business unless the UK got its way. But in the midst of the Falklands crisis, the major EEC states adroitly shattered the British presumption. They voted through agricultural price increases over the protests of the UK representatives, who claimed this was against the rules. To no avail: the UK's domestic sovereignty was decisively violated, as Europe decided upon a rise in British food prices against the wishes of London. Already committed in the South Atlantic, Thatcher could not afford to be belligerent on two fronts. This was fortunate, as a conflict with the EEC would have pressed on the country's genuine economic weakness. So when she was asked in Parliament whether she 'would continue to want Britain to be a member of the EEC', Thatcher's response was: 'I am suggesting that we do not dash into any hurried conclusions before we have had time to think these things out'.[7] There are some wars, it seems, you do not enter lightly.

Unlike the dash to the South Atlantic. It can be argued that Thatcher was a prisoner of events (in that she might not have survived either a motion of censure or an enquiry if she had not gone to war), while in a larger sense Parliament's Churchillism thrust her into a demonstration of her 'Iron' capacities. Certainly she could not have successfully grabbed the mantle of Churchill single-handed, such a deed would have been fiercely contested by his other inheritors. But that said, she did not need time 'to think things out'; it was the kind of issue she had wanted all along. If Galtieri was obliged to gamble on an invasion for reasons of domestic politics—under imminent threat of a general strike and faced with outspoken opposition—then what was political necessity for him was a godsend to his British counterpart. And not merely because the Falklands were a spectacular diversion from the economic indices and the rise of the SDP. Equally important was the opportunity for a display of pure ideological fortitude. The nothingness of the islands gave Thatcher perfect scope for action. Not a part of Europe, not integral to the Cold War, not even of economic consequence—the Falklands were a perfect stage for the exercise of *Principle* because they were so utterly removed from the complications of substance. Here, at last, was a way of showing 'who governed' to general admiration, in an antipodean nowhere that could be isolated by hunter-killer submarines. Just as Mao said because the Chinese people were poor and blank, beautiful pictures could be drawn upon them; so the blankness of the Falklands allowed the 'lessons' of Thatcherism to be projected onto them with perfect clarity.

But if the pedagogy is designed for the general erudition of the British public, the point is being driven home with peculiar force against Thatcher's enemies in the Conservative Party. The rise of Thatcherism signals an interesting mutation in the political direction of the main ruling-class party. Thatcher's sword may have cut leftwards only, but it has done so from a point so far on the right that its initial victims have been in the centre and top of the Tory Party itself.

Just before her election, Thatcher distinguished herself from her Labour opponents and Conservative predecessors thus: 'I'm not a consensus politician or a pragmatic politician, I'm a conviction politician.'[8] The difference is more than one of style, and even that is important. The form of dominance she offers is novel not only in terms of government since 1945, but also vis à vis the Conservatives and the long hegemony of Baldwin. It is interesting to compare her to Churchill himself. The old warrior would have looked askance upon the evangelical grocer's daughter. Especially, perhaps, upon the way that she conducts war. Criticizing the American approach to international conflict, Churchill stated,

> The British mind does not work quite in this way. We do not think that logic and clear-cut principles are necessarily the sole keys to what ought to be done in swiftly changing and indefinable situations. In war in particular, we assigned a larger importance to opportunism and improvisation, seeking rather to live and conquer in accordance with the unfolding event than to aspire to dominate it often by fundamental decisions.[9]

This is a wonderful description of Albion's perfidy by one of its master practitioners. Bluff, opportunism, the subordination of all principles to the national interest of the moment: Churchill was describing the pragmatic flexibility of force and fraud by which the Empire was made and which has confounded so many people around the world.

Thatcher, with her insistent emphasis on the governing principles of her foreign policy, is not exactly the true inheritor of Churchill's bellicosity. But nor was Churchill *merely* what the Thatcherites would term a 'wet'. That aspect of his legacy in which pragmatism is all, was characteristically summed up by Macmillan: 'In the long run, and for the common good, the umpire is better than the duel.'[10] (It was a justification for his 'soft' policy towards the unions.) While Macmillan took the pragmatic wing of the Conservative wartime policy to its logical conclusion, Thatcher has taken off on the other wing alone. How far will it fly?

When Thatcher gained the nominal leadership of the Conservatives in 1975, her front-bench was overwhelmingly hostile, having initially supported Heath. It took Thatcher two years even after she won the 1979 election, to bring the cabinet fully under her control and that took all her considerable skill and contempt. Her general attitude towards her senior colleagues is apparently summed up by her description of the cabinet as 'my blue bunnies'.[11] When there were signs of rebellion in the hutch, she moved promptly. The turning point came in September 1981. To understand its full drama, the history of the Heath years must be recalled. He had originally pledged to remove the state from day-to-day economic matters. But after his initial setbacks, he reverted to a more activist stance in what was dubbed his 'U-turn'. With Thatcher in office, the Left feared an immediate, savage assault on the working-class institutions which would outdo Heath's, while the media commentators waited with cynical smiles for her Heath-like return to more pragmatic and sensible policies after an initial brush with reality. Both groups were disconcerted. Whereas Heath had set out to *renovate* the traditional British patrician class in a European context and to reinforce its perspectives with a more intelligent globalism, Thatcher set out to *replace* the old paternalists altogether, with their attachment to 'consensus' policies and social welfare. This, indeed, seems to have been her prime task, and so she cautiously backed away from union showdowns she might lose, in particular with the miners, without abandoning her objectives.

In the summer of 1981, the effects of economic deflation began to alarm the 'wets'. Lord Thorneycroft, Chairman of the Conservative Party, suggested that there should not be an Autumn reshuffle. This was seen as a move to protect the old guard's numerical majority in the Cabinet. Thatcher was apparently annoyed. In September 1981,

Thorneycroft was removed as Party Chairman and replaced by one of her associates from the back-benches, Cecil Parkinson, educated at a state school. Lord Soames and Sir Ian Gilmour were dismissed. James Prior, who was the 'wet' Secretary of State for Employment, was shunted off to Northern Ireland—a graveyard of political careers—and replaced by another self-made Thatcherite, Norman Tebbitt, who began to draft anti-union laws. The *Mail* and the *Express* gloated over the fall of the 'grandees'. Thus, far from softening her policies in mid-term, Thatcher reinforced her original partisan direction. Gilmour said that she was steering the country straight onto the rocks (not a reference to the Falklands) and called for an amelioration of her relentless deflation. One commentator concluded: 'The old Tory establishment must know now, if it did not know before, that it faces ultimate liquidation at Thatcher's hands if she stays as Leader.'[12]

The war in the South Atlantic may now have ensured Thatcher's predominance. Lord Carrington, the patrician Foreign Secretary, resigned after the Junta's take-over, to the delight of the bellicose MPs. More important, Britain's ultimate victory appeared to vindicate Thatcher's adamantine, anti-consensus politics. A discernible shift to the right took place in the Conservative Party as a result of the war. Immediately after the surrender at Port Stanley, the *Financial Times*' political editor concluded, 'The Tory grandees are on their way out'.[13] The rightwards movement might well continue, and he noted ominously, 'The Prime Minister's views on law and order, for example, have yet to be given full expression'. A week later *The Times* agreed, 'The old guard have largely been routed'.[14]

If this is indeed the case, then the Falklands crisis will have made a historic contribution to Britain's domestic politics. In class terms, Thatcher represents the self-made, ideological believer in country and capitalism for whom exchange and the market have precedence over manufacture. Under her leadership, petty-bourgeois militancy has taken over from the old, semi-cultured, patrician elite. Has the governess now taken over from the squire? The question might seem an odd way to address the Falklands War for those who are not British. Yet within the UK it is a recognizable interpretation of the dispatch of the Armada. The country house has at last been captured. But it has not been stormed by an aroused rabble of gardeners, against whom it was well fortified. It has not been taken over by the disgruntled servants, who have always been closely policed. It has not been seized by a radicalized scion of the mansion who had the misfortune to be repelled by its inequality and attracted to theory. It has not even been overrun by the proletariat, who are kept a good distance away. Assault from all these likely quarters had been foreseen and was defused. Instead, the pillar of rectitude and narrow-mindedness, the governess whose loyalty had never been questioned, who naively *believes* in the whole thing and regards it as virtuous, has decided to run it herself.

Twenty years ago it was argued that the historic origins of the British crisis lay in the stultification of its bourgeois revolution by a capitalist aristocracy at once landed and schooled in world dominion.[15] There may be much in the argument that needs to be up-dated or corrected, certainly in so far as it presumed a model of 'proper' bourgeois revolution on the European mainland. It would be more accurate to say that capitalism is necessarily a system in which economic power does not rule directly. It therefore never finds a completely coherent, organic expression of its dominion in any country. The economic 'democracy' of capital, its necessary freedom to accumulate competitively, will always ensure that its institutions of legislation and of executive political power are independent of, as well as subordinate to, money. Nonetheless, the central argument remains compelling. Historically dominated by financial capital located in the south, whose millionaires always outnumbered industrial barons, the British state was animated by those trained in an imperial rather than a domestic role, and in ledgers and fields rather than in factories. The result has been a *marked* absence of a recognizable bourgeois political class in any dominant sense—at once practical, realistic and—yes—businesslike.

Thatcher's own intellectual guru, Sir Keith Joseph, recognized this, when he suggested that one source of Britain's economic problems was that it 'never had a capitalist ruling class or a stable *haute bourgeoisie*'.[16] But the Thatcherites themselves have hardly filled the gap. The contest between them and the 'wets' for the leadership of the Conservative Party and the nation will not resolve the structural weakness. It is a struggle between a supra-bourgeois and a sub-bourgeois stratum; between stricken patricians and over-confident *arrivistes*. It is important to note the limits as well as the significance of this shift, one which has only altered the balance of power within the same class bloc. The squire may have been superannuated, to return to the metaphor, but he is still allowed to poke the embers from the comfort of his armchair. He has not been ejected, nor has the house been burnt down. In particular, Thatcherism has if anything invigorated the relationship with the City and its foreign investments which are so lucrative for those with money at a time when the country as a whole is in recession.[17]

The domestic transformation of the Conservative Party helps to explain a paradox, one which puzzled a number of foreigners. Why, after the UK has given away territory many times its own size since 1945, should it baulk and strain at the Falklands, islands remarkable for their insignificance? As if to underline the contrast, when the Navy set sail for the South Atlantic, the Queen flew to Canada to sign the formal assignation of that country's sovereignty into its own hands. Because Canada's dominion status was historically early, residual powers over its constitution had remained in London. The ceremonial events of the new, 1982 Constitution were boycotted by Quebec, while the document itself ignored the just claims of the Indians with whom the Crown had originally treatied. All the same, the celebrations were a further symbol of that peaceful handover which has been much touted as the acme of British reasonableness or even proof of the British civilizing mission, despite innumerable armed interventions. Indeed, negotiated relinquishment has functioned as a retrospective vindication of the British Empire. For even when it has been a consequence of duress, implemented to prevent a military debacle, final agreement has always helped to incorporate some of the local elite and head off subsequent hostility, thus preserving many British economic interests. The only outright failure was in South Yemen. It was hardly sufficient to undo the image of a historic and elegant transition.

Yet now the best part of the Royal Navy has been dispatched to prevent Argentina from retaining that which it has already been offered implicitly, namely sovereignty over the Falkland Islands. The response is further evidence of the decline of the 'patricians' and a step that helps eliminate their influence. For it was the British mercantile gentry (such as Macmillan) just as much as the public school reformers like Attlee, who had overseen and manipulated the ductile transfer of sovereignty around the world. They bowed to the winds of change, and this helped Britain to retain disproportionate influence as its economic power waned. Perhaps their most outstanding representative was Lord Mountbatten, a relative of the Royal Family, Allied Supreme Commander for Southeast Asia during the Second World War and the Labour appointed Governor of India, who presided over the sub-continent's independence. Although no one should underestimate its recuperative powers, Lord Carrington, the architect of the Zimbabwe settlement, was probably the last representative of this caste to wield independent influence from high office. He resigned from his post as Foreign Minister after the 3 April Falklands debate, in which his policies were denounced from both sides of the House of Commons but never defended by his Cabinet colleagues. The tenor of his own statement in the House of Lords—which also debated the Falklands on 3 April—was noticeably different from that of Thatcher's. Their Lordships were saddened rather than enraged. Meanwhile, in the 'other place', Poujadists of imperialism took command of foreign policy, and this may come to be seen as one of the more significant aspects of the Falklands affair.

It was not completely fortuitous that the Falklands should have suddenly precipitated a conflict between the Thatcherites and the wets. Surprisingly enough, the islands have been a matter in which the Prime Minister took a personal interest. The standard uninformed view at the beginning of the crisis (which I also shared) blamed the problem on the uninspired approach of the Foreign Office. Edward Pearce, a leader writer for the *Daily Telegraph* put it as follows. All would have been well, and Argentina would not have dared an invasion, if Britain had made it plain that it would literally stick to its guns in the Falklands. On the other hand, 'Had we been ruthlessly soft instead of soft in the fair-minded and gentlemanly way we prefer, the Falklanders would have been told that time was up, grants for resettlement in New Zealand were available ...'. However, as he imagined it, the Foreign Office tried to bluff. Its representatives talked about leaseback, in their 'maddeningly unassailable way', which Pearce thinks Thatcher is right to detest. The Foreign Office thus occupied 'the worst of all possible worlds'.[18] We now know that this explanation, which blames the 'wets' and sees Thatcher as coming to the rescue to salvage British pride, is wrong.

The Foreign Office in fact conducted a remarkably successful, long-term strategy across changing administrations to persuade the islanders to come to a *modus vivendi* with Argentina. Since 1968 relations with the mainland had been improved deliberately. In 1980, Ridley (Eton and Balliol, but by no means a wet) argued that the time had come precisely to be tough with the islanders. But Thatcher over-ruled him (gave him a 'mauling').[19] It appears that *she* did not want to 'lose' the islands and, if the *Economist* account is correct, her intervention frustrated exactly the kind of 'ruthless softness' Pearce suggests would have worked. Nonetheless, the British continued to negotiate with Argentina even when it was in fact doing so in bad faith. Carrington told the Lords on 3 April that negotiations with an Argentinian representative in New York on 27 February 1982, 'seemed to have reached agreement on a satisfactory basis for further negotiations'. A message had come from him to which Carrington was 'preparing a reply'. Could it have been that its composition was proving difficult?

For it transpires that at the beginning of February Thatcher personally signed a letter to a Tory activist to reassure her that the withdrawal of the *Endurance* from patrol off the Falklands would not place the islands at risk. Furthermore, she wrote, 'The wishes of the Falkland Islanders are paramount. The Government has no intention of entering into a solution to the dispute with Argentina which is not acceptable to the islanders and to Parliament.'[20] Had this been so bluntly put to the Argentinian negotiators in New York, it seems most unlikely that they would have felt a satisfactory basis for further talks had been achieved. There seems, then, to have been a contradiction between the UK's actual and diplomatic positions, one due not to the wetness of the Foreign Office or to the toughness of Thatcher but to the imposition of the latter on the former. This was then multiplied by a further twist. Two weeks before the invasion, Carrington asked for a submarine to be sent to the Falklands and a Cabinet committee chaired by Thatcher rejected the proposal, at least according to a report in the *Observer*.[21] Thatcher's determination to cut back on expenditure meant that she was unwilling to wield the stick, even though *her* policy on the Falklands was intransigent. If this sequence of events is approximately accurate, it is not surprising that Thatcher fears the outcome of the Franks' inquiry, which is now investigating the circumstances of Argentina's invasion.

Indeed, she attempted to displace attention away from her own administration by proposing an inquiry into the previous twenty years. An angry intervention by Heath prevented this, when he attacked Thatcher for wanting to 'rummage' through his government's papers to keep the limelight away from her own.[22] Heath's outburst must also have been motivated by frustration. For he had earlier suggested that Argentina should be left 'a way out', only to be shouted down by Thatcherite Falkland warriors on the Conservative benches. Now that she had scored her victory, Heath's own prospects for an influential role as elder statesman in the Party seemed definitely blighted.

A phenomenon like Thatcherism is defined and shaped by those who oppose it in the present as much as by its relationship with the past. Thatcher seems to regard the Social Democrats under Roy Jenkins as her most dangerous opponents. It is they who seek to fulfil the task projected by Edward Heath: the SDP is that lost tribe of British politics, a bourgeois political party. The two major planks of SDP policy, a genuine attachment to Europe (which none of the others share) and a commitment to proportional representation, are both signs of this. The latter especially, should it become reality, will break the grip of the first-past-the-post system of Parliamentary election, and thereby crack the hold of the present incumbents. Nonetheless, despite its assault on the 'old system', the SDP is ambivalent in its basic attitudes. Although the most 'realistic' contender for power, it remains at one and the same time the most radical and the most conservative party.

The conservative element is obvious enough, in effect it seeks a coalition of the centre. In the 1950s, the word 'Butskellism' stood for the social and economic policies of two successive Labour and Conservative Chancellors, Gaitskell and Butler, each of whom sought to become, and nearly became, Prime Minister. The SDP seeks to put a Butskellite Premier finally into office. The majority of the SDP MPs (almost all of them defectors from the Labour benches) come from this stable and its opportunist variations. For them, the Party's slogan of 'breaking the mould' is merely a neat item of campaign rhetoric, a way of cashing in on the electorate's desire for the new, in order to *preserve* their parliamentary seats, the old fix-it consensus politics and Britain itself, from the influence of 'the extremists of left and right'. The shock of the Falklands crisis for this predominantly Parliamentary wing of the SDP was considerable. After a year of stunning by-election successes, in which at one point their support in the polls had touched 50% of the electorate, they lost two successive by-elections and their local election results were appalling: their apparently invincible record had been stymied by the mould itself breaking all records. How could a party which in alliance with the Liberals promised a new national consensus fare anything but badly when an all-party national consensus had hauled up the Union Jack?

Another wing of the SDP really does want radical change: it seeks a genuine modernization of Britain politically, its attachment to Europe is cultural as well as commercial. This tendency within the SDP offered the best mainstream criticism of the war. In the *Financial Times* (6 May), Samuel Brittain, a monetarist of SDP leaning, wrote a fine piece after the sinking of the *Belgrano*, titled 'Stop the Killing Straightaway'. The *Guardian*'s regular columnist Peter Jenkins was easily the most consistent and hard-hitting critic of the Armada and its effects on Britain's international and domestic politics, and condemned the enterprise from the outset. Anthony Sampson expressed cautious scepticism in *Newsweek* (7 June). The *London Review of Books* (which has endorsed the SDP) published Dalyell and also Raymond Williams against the war. It was significant, however, that the *London Review of Books* had to turn to a Labour MP and a socialist writer, rather than to any of the SDP members in the House of Commons. There, the gung-ho Dr Owen was deemed to have had a 'good war' and to have emerged as a credible leader of the new party. He stood against Jenkins in the first SDP leadership ballot and with significant press support gained 40% of the vote.

Today there is talk of a possible early election in which Thatcher could cash in her gains over the Falklands. The future of the islands themselves could then become an issue between the Prime Minister and the SDP, and if her own position proves the more popular, Britain might become the prisoner of her 'Iron Will' internationally. The question is whether Argentina should have anything more to do with the Falklands, as if this were a matter for the UK to decide. At the beginning of June, as British troops were poised for their by then inevitable victory, Thatcher was pressed about American desires for a show of some 'magnanimity'. She bristled at the idea. Dismissing any future for Argentina on the islands, she declared that the islanders 'have been loyal to us, we must be loyal to them', and stated that anything less than this would mean 'treachery and betrayal of our own people'. At the same time a convenient new theme came into prominence from the 'front line' itself. Max Hastings of the *Express* group wrote (2 June), 'I think that the only outcome of the war which would cause great bitterness among those who are fighting is any peace that gives Argentina a share in governing the Falklands after we have won'. Thatcher's attitude, with its witch-hunting mentality, its innuendo, its lack of proportion and its presumption that she could define treason to her own liking, came under attack from Peter Jenkins.[23] Meanwhile in *The Times* (4 June), Roy Jenkins had insisted that 'a negotiated settlement is essential after victory ... the fact is that we cannot guarantee both the long-term military security and economic viability of the Falklands'. One feels like saying, 'Now he tells us!'[24] Jenkins was shrewd enough to meet the key arguments against Thatcher. British blood could not determine subsequent policy or 'British valour would become the enemy of British interest'. The phrase demonstrated fine literary craftsmanship and should be inscribed in the pocketbook of every soldier. He also proceeded to assail the born-again Churchillians of the Falkland episode: to suggest that it 'amounts to a national regeneration comparable to 1940 ... shows a pathetic lack of proportion'. It was as if the debate was taking place across the globe, for Hastings filed a report four days later in which he quoted a colour-sergeant, 'If a place is worth dying for, it's got to be worth keeping'. His paper endorsed the attitude in an editorial: the *Express* (8 June) came out for a 'Fortress Falklands' under the UK's perpetual sovereignty.

On its own terms this argument will have a bearing on future relations with the United States, as Washington seeks to mend relations with Argentina that were damaged by its support for Thatcher in the Falklands. The domestic repercussions may be greater, however. In politics, especially in British politics today, nothing is certain. But Thatcher's unilateral arbitration of British destiny in the South Atlantic for her own political ends threatens to bring a new melody into the UK. Foreign issues have long played a crucial role in domestic affairs, since the battle over Irish Home Rule a century ago. Often these issues crystalize existing divisions and rebound onto the electorate at second hand. A good example of this was when Gaitskell imposed teeth and spectacle charges in

April 1951 in a budget designed to meet expenditures entailed by British participation in the Korean war. Bevan resigned in protest and the Labour Party was split, which contributed to its electoral defeat later in the year. However, despite the role that such disputes over international relations have played, in electoral terms there has been a bi-partisan consensus on foreign policy since 1940, with the sole exception of Suez. From the American alliance to the Common Market, the nature of inter-party debate could be summed up by Eden's phrase about his attitude towards Bevin's conduct as Minister for Foreign Affairs after 1945: 'I would publically have agreed with him more, if I had not been anxious to embarrass him less.'[25]

What if Thatcher challenges the other parties on their attitude towards the Falklands, as an election issue? For the *Financial Times* (16 June), a permanent garrison on the islands is a foolish 'grandiose, imperial gesture'. Likewise for Jenkins and the SDP. Neither the Social Democrats nor Labour will feel comfortable if Thatcher attempts to garner the imperial sentiments excited by her victory in the Falklands war. Not only has her resolution in the South Atlantic apparently confirmed her domination over the Conservative 'wets', it now threatens to polarize electoral politics through 1983. 'Little Englandism' was successfully stifled by the political operators at Westminster when such sentiments threatened to block entry into the Common Market. But now, 'Great Britishness' might be released by the Falklands in such a way that it cannot be rebottled. The subjects of the Crown have never yet been allowed to decide the geopolitical destiny of the British Isles, but Thatcherism may be poised to break this ordinance, just as it appealed successfully over the heads of the 'grandees' to the ranks of Tory opinion.

The left will be especially tested if Parliamentary nationalism comes to the fore electorally. There is no need to stress the distinctiveness of Tony Benn. Himself a modernizing socialist radicalized by high Cabinet office, he has become the spokesman for a Labour rank and file who have also rejected the miseries of Labour policies in office. They desire a socialist programme at once committed and accountable. Although this has yet to gain any popular approval, Bennism originally had a different source of attraction. It spoke against the EEC. After 1970, Benn's resistance to British affiliation helped Labour to appear, during the Heath years, as the more 'national' of the two parties. Subsequently, the Bennite programme of economic nationalism, protective tariffs, exit from the EEC, made it a dangerous if still improbable national alternative. Now Thatcher has trumped the left on the national question, as she has run up the Union Jack over monetarism, unemployment and the free export of capital. Those who warned that should Labour ever take the UK out of the EEC, it would lead to a triumph for the Right, seem to be vindicated.[26] The Tories have demonstrated that they can build a nationalist alliance across class, region and party, with virtuoso speed and panache. Just as Foot found his endorsement of the Task Force taken from him by Thatcher with a gusto he could never match, so Benn, or just as likely a Labour rightist like Peter Shore, would find themselves trumped by Powellism, should they begin to sever London's relations with Brussels.

The scenario may be implausible, but the argument is crucial. In a recent issue of *Tribune* (11 June) towards the end of the Falklands campaign, its editor explained why all socialists should join the Labour Party: 'The truth is that Labour has everything to gain from adopting a radical programme. For months every opinion poll has been telling us that public opinion is overwhelmingly hostile to the Common Market and the American bomb.' Note well, not the British bomb. The public's attitude is veritably isolationist. Thatcher has drawn on these *same* sentiments to garner support for her Falklands War. Indeed much of the Left lined up behind her, and if this company did not include the editor of *Tribune* who denounced the 'Falklands madness', nonetheless he has still not seen quite how large is the writing on the wall. Benn's opposition to the Armada however, has given him a new profile. By discarding his greatest apparent asset—nationalism—the opportunism of much of his public image has been transformed into courage. By saying that the fleet should be turned back, without any argument as to the 'rightfulness' of its objectives, Benn seems to have come across as practical and understandable and no more unpopular. At last the Left may now have broken from its Churchillist impress and if this can be made good it could well mark not a 'historic compromise' but a historic breakthrough.

In the wake of her Falklands triumph and her stirring speeches in celebration of the 'spirit of the South Atlantic', Thatcher's politics have taken on a clearer and more definable outline. Her monetarism was always a bit of a puzzle because the Conservative party dislikes ideologists of any kind. How did she manage to appear unideological herself and avoid the Party's hostility in this regard, while remaining so attached to her 'principles'? The answer, we can now see, is that Thatcher is not an ideologist in the proper sense. She is not deeply wedded to new ideas or even old ones; her ideal has been to remain 'true' to the past and to its supposedly simple values. By firming up traditional Tory suspicion of theory, she has made an 'ideology' of the prejudice against ideology itself, in particular against the ideas of the wartime consensus. Thatcher's rejoicing in military victory as the beginning of the Great British renaissance reveals, then, an almost uncontrolled nostalgia. She doesn't display a realistic commitment to 'cut the country's cloth to fit', to use the language she reserves for the working class. Rather, she is cutting the country to fit her costume.

The feebleness of her actual programme of renewal as it appears today is matched by the ruthlessness of her dedication to the destruction of many of the gains that have been made in Britain since the war, both economically and in the quality of life. Yet the double irrationality of Thatcherism should not lead us to presume that it will lack continued popularity. The failure of Churchillism to provide either a right-wing, a left-wing or a centrist formation capable of directing a sustained modernization, has led to the rise of Thatcher. Her standpoint is the past's vision of the past. From it she has delivered her terrible rebuke to the failures of the present. Nonetheless, her strident judgements have addressed 'real problems, real and lived experiences, real contradictions'.[27] Her 'authoritarian populism' strikes a chord, while Foot's Labour patriotism is ill-dressed and unconvincing. Although Thatcher's domestic policies have ensured a degree of social and economic fear amongst the working classes unequalled since 1945, she has also managed to address directly some of the aspirations and beliefs which the electorate hold. The Labour Party leaders, by contrast, seem so bowed down by their years of 'responsible' government, that while they may speak more 'sense', they give the impression that they address only the managers, civil servants and owners while having abandoned any attempt to win popular assent to their own programme. It does not follow that Labour cannot win an election in the future. Its leaders appear to be banking on a reprieve that comes from mass repugnance at the costs of Thatcher's policies. But whether or not this proves a successful calculation, it has been motivated in good part by the Labour leadership's inability and unwillingness to generate positive support—starting within its own party—for the policies and solutions it offers.

This brings us to the question of the 'rationality' of Thatcherism. To what extent are her policies intelligent ones for the British state, and to what degree is she really the prisoner of its decline rather than the inspirer of its liberation? Alan Freeman, for example, has criticised Benn's rhetoric that the UK is becoming like a Third World country, a semi-developed colony of multi-national capitalism. On the contrary, Freeman asserts that Britain holds overseas assets of $84 billion. It remains the second greatest power in terms of global investment and has the West's second largest overseas military as well. The cost of these two commitments are the key cause of the British decline, in his view.[28] Yet they are also, it seems, the expression of its strength. Presumably the combination is a vicious one. As the decline continues, the relative influence of the military, the City and multinational interests grows vis à vis the domestic economy and society. Thatcherism could be seen as the expression of this tendency to reduce the British Isles themselves into a Task Force: its non-redundant population conscripted and its working industry requisitioned for the overseas adventures of its masters.

Yet there is something unconvincing about this picture. For the expanded role of the City as an international financial centre needs depoliticization more than anything. Switzerland is surely the model, and policies that threaten to politicize the role of the City run the risk of undermining its international position, hence its unwillingness to impose too stringent sanctions upon Buenos Aires. In other words, the military over-extension of the British state, while it may share the same origins as the financial globalism of the City, could now be an impediment to the latter's interests. Indeed the reason for the UK's refusal to formally declare war on Argentina may have been related to this tension. The *State Research* group has pointed out in its *Bulletin* No. 30, that a legal declaration of war would have had severe commercial consequences for the City.

But if this is true, did any special interests encourage Britain to go to war with Argentina over the Falklands? Undoubtedly there was a strong Navy lobby at work behind the scenes. In addition, it was said that there are fabulous resources underneath the Antarctic ice, there is oil off the Falklands as well. Could this be why the Armada was sent? To secure for Great Britain a slice of the immense riches of the far southern hemisphere, now waiting to be tapped? The question seems to gain force when the size and efficiency of the Falklands lobby is considered. Nine MPs are members of the United Kingdom Falkland Islands Committee—about one MP for less than 100 families on the Islands themselves, an extraordinary ratio.[29] Evidently, the MPs must be interested in something else, apart from the actual inhabitants. The Falkland Islands Company helped to establish the Committee in 1968 and contributes to its funds. Here then, it seems, is a powerful financial interest that seeks to sustain Parliamentary allegiance to the South Atlantic. The oddity, however, is that something that is the opposite of a conspiracy of gain may have been at work, for the Company was moving to improve its now profitable relations with Buenos Aires. It was nostalgia for one of the last colonies and dreams of Empire rather than base calculation that attracted MPs to the Falkland lobby.

Evidence of this can be seen in the more serious discussions of the resource potential of the Falklands. The Shackleton Report, for example, which will be considered in Chapter 7, was primarily concerned with such an assessment.

Its conclusions were cautious. The value and accessibility of the off-shore oil around the Islands have probably been exaggerated, in its view. Although oil probably does exist under the surrounding waters, the surface conditions are worse than those of the North Sea, while the location is much further removed from major centres of consumption. The costs of extraction, therefore, might prove exhorbitant. Only one thing was absolutely certain, the Report stressed. No development of the oil reserves would be possible without the co-operation of Argentina. The risks of contested sovereignty would scare off potential investors while the logistic problems alone dictated the need for Argentinian collaboration. Hence, in Shackleton's view, a resolution of the sovereignty issue and political stability were the pre-condition for future economic development on any scale. An oil lobby then, which desired to profit from the zone's potential, would have pushed for a settlement with Buenos Aires, not further contest and certainly not a clash of arms. If anything, the Foreign Office was doing its best to assuage such business interests. The oil lobby—and who can doubt that such exists?—was almost certainly *against* the war.

It does not follow that the idea of oil and other riches did not have its effect upon the behaviour of MPs. The ultra-patriots of the House of Commons were in search of a cause. What could make them seem more farsighted than predictions about the value of the krill in the South Atlantic—the high protein types of prawn on which the whales once used to feed? The capacity of parliamentarians to be impressed by fatuous ideas has always been notable. Tories who scorn Marxism for its base approach to politics think nothing of wheeling out ludicrous economic arguments to justify their beliefs. By this behaviour they do indeed pose a certain problem for materialists. For it is evident that the MPs are not 'objectively determined' by such notions. Edward du Cann who referred to the 'substantial treasures' of the South Atlantic in the special Saturday debate of 3 April, was no closer to a balance sheet of Antarctic assets than any old gossip down the road. His real concern was not the potential wealth but the idea that it was *British*: Whatever it was out there, it should be ours. Despite its economic form, his argument was the pure expression of a political culture.

A further example of the fantastical notions which possessed the Falklands lobby in the Commons came on 20 May. In that day's debate, David Atkinson, the Conservative MP for Bournemouth East, spoke in support of Thatcher. (Sir John Eden who spoke on 3 April represents Bournmouth West; obviously Bournmouth takes a great interest in the Falklands.) The world does not trade with Britain and buy its goods, Atkinson pointed out, because the products of the UK were better in quality than West Germany's or cheaper than those offered by Japan. Why then, did *anyone* purchase goods from the UK? 'Countries ... trade with us still because of other qualities for which we are peculiar as a nation—qualities which we are now displaying and principles which we are now defending'.[30] This is a new version of 'trade follows the flag'; British products will be sought after and imported despite the fact that they are both over-expensive and poor in quality because, when push comes to shove in the Falklands or elsewhere, the lion still barks .... These 'economic' arguments, we can see, are merely a pretence. Their aim is to coat the unbusinesslike behaviour of British politics with a veneer of economic realism.

In Chapter 3, I wrote that when the MPs debated the Falklands on 3 April, they looked at the South Atlantic through the eyes of Churchill and believed that they too 'would put the Great back into Britain'. I thought about this phrase, and discussed it with others. Was it not too cheap a shot and too glib a description? Perhaps I was pushing my case too far, and thus weakening its impact. Then, on the evening of the victory at Port Stanley, Thatcher emerged from No 10 to say, 'Today has put the Great back into Britain'. Later, as we have seen, she claimed in her Cheltenham speech that Britain is still the country that once ruled a quarter of the globe. Thatcher has overseen an acceleration in the relative decline of the UK compared to other second level powers. Yet she has asserted a Churchillian renaissance that has wonderfully transported the country back into becoming a world power once again.

Thatcherism can be regarded as a new variant, if a more extreme one, of the mind-set that has held all British politicians in its grip since 1945. For if the crippling aspect of Churchillism were to be summed up in one sentence, it is that British politicians have been unable to articulate a programme of reform for the UK as a minor industrial power except in terms that seek to reassert Britain's *world* greatness. The roots of this over-ambition, one that has led government after government to under-achievement, lies in the wartime conflation, when the country was saved in the name of the Empire. There are two different aspects to the British collapse then; in both of which it should be noted the military has played a role. The first is the vertiginous decline of the United Kingdom from its role as a world power to a position in the cluster of second rank placemen. This actually took place during the Second World War, indeed one could argue that its defining event was the expulsion of the expeditionary force from Europe at Dunkirk. It was fully revealed by the Suez crisis in 1956, when Moscow threatened to rocket-bomb London and Washington used its financial leverage to impose a humiliating withdrawal. The end of London's role as the centre of a planetary empire was the consequence of *external* change:

it was bound to come however skilled and far-sighted its leaders might have been, because the rest of the world could never be subordinated to its dictation. But while this definitive and irreversible fall was brought about by forces beyond Britain's power, it has been compounded since 1945 by an additional type of decline. The UK has 'become one of the weakest and least successful of the second rate powers'.[31]

Here we find the second and 'unnecessary' aspect of the collapse. That Britain would cease to be a global power was inevitable. That it had also to become an economic cripple compared to other European states was not. The rational task of modernization in Britain is to transform its society into a relatively thriving and prosperous *second* rank country that might achieve the standard of living of, say, Holland. But this apparently modest ambition—one which today would nonetheless mean doubling the national product—is far too modest for the politicians of Westminster. For them, to say that one wants the UK to be a northern European country like the others, is virtually treason. Britishness, the national essence, demands *much* more, in their view.

Ironically, one of the keywords with which many express this compression of the two aspects of the British decline is 'appeasement'. The collapse of British power is somehow blamed upon the weak-willed Chamberlain along with his supporters, and now their latter day reincarnations in the Foreign Office. The decline and fall of the Empire was due to a failure of will and a culture of insouciance in this view. Of course there is at least an iota of truth to the argument, which describes the style in which the decline was conducted. But by placing the blame for the termination of Britain's global role on a domestic failure of the spirit, it is implicitly suggested that if only the British could now act differently, one could resuscitate the bygone greatness. Condemnations of 'appeasement' today—in the context of the Parliamentary nation—have buried within them an assertion of past world power as somehow still an actual potential for Westminster.[32]

No major British politician has yet commanded any support for denouncing the lure of the old glories. Many in the UK might be receptive to such an appeal. Perhaps part of the positive response Thatcher has elicited when she demands sacrifice is a 'popular realism' that is far more up to date than hers. But the dominant mode of expression remains bound to Churchillism. Successive governments seek to defend the diminished position of Britain by striving for its old and irretrievable position. Anthony Eden expressed his determination to wrest back the Suez Canal, by insisting that Nasser was the reincarnation of Hitler. Macmillan sought a place for himself as one of the 'Big Three' alongside

Kennedy and Kruschev. Harold Wilson, within a month of taking office as Prime Minister told the City of London Lord Mayor's banquet, 'We are a world power and a world influence, or we are nothing'.[33] He was attacking racialism in the Midlands, but the sentiment illuminated an all party feeling. Seven years later Edward Heath defended his government's successful application to join the Common Market in these terms: 'We have the chance of a new greatness, we must go in if we want to remain Great Britain, and take the chance of becoming Greater Britain'.[34] Similarly, the task that the united House of Commons gave to Margaret Thatcher on 3 April was to defend and preserve the national fantasy of Britain's global destiny. And when Thatcher rejoiced over the Falklands victory, she welcomed precisely her ability to lay claim to the 'Great' tradition.

While all the wise leaders of the Kingdom see it as their task to ensure that Britain remains 'Great', and while the population votes for those who seem most plausible in this theatre, it seems that the decline bestowed by Churchillism is destined to continue.

The self-punishing ambition has been expressed above all in terms of excessive military expenditure. Today the British habit of mocking soldiers has turned sour. The celebration of coercion which accompanied the Falklands Armada shows every sign of returning to the United Kingdom. It is a theme that Thatcher sought from the beginning of her leadership of the Conservative Party. The 'Iron Lady' initially directed her ferrous gaze eastwards towards the bear. She was presumably mortified when few took this seriously. Now she has gained the belligerent nationalist colours that her policies always needed to appear to succeed. For behind the hardness of Thatcher's approach there is a commitment to the market rather than production. She is not concerned about getting the country to work, rather she wants its services to work well. *Rules*, not output, are what she is attached to, and ultimately the possibility of positive regimentation lies behind such a perspective. Militarization might well become domesticated in a way that has been missing from Britain hitherto. Soldiers have always paraded in central London, but in colourful uniforms and as a tourist attraction rather than a warning to the population. For a decade in Ireland, the forces have had an altogether more ominous and unattractive role. Now, the military may be projected as one of the few agencies who can 'get things done'. The reference to the 'coolly professional British forces' in the *Economist* is a possible warning. What if the Falklands fail to give the nation its needed 'surge' of self-confidence? What if the country is so churlish and ungrateful not to work hard enough? Might not this be construed as a betrayal of those who have sacrificed their lives for the British way of life? Perhaps a bit of that cool professionalism will have to be applied at home, to 'liberate' the mainland itself from the legacy of the 'progressive consensus' Thatcher denounced in 1975 ... Whatever one might think of that possibility, there can be little doubt that Thatcher's form of Churchillism has been to turn against its social legacy the name of Churchill himself. The more she succeeds, the more all other tendencies in British political life will have to undertake their own reckoning with the past.

Margaret Thatcher granted a special interview to the *Daily Express* on 26 July. 'It was understood right from the outset that the honour of our people and our country was at stake', she said about the Falklands. Success there she continued, has 'boosted Britain in the international world colossally'. It was a revealing emphasis: it was neither the Kelpers nor the islands that mattered so much as British pride. As for the Conservative Party it shows that what is needed is 'not consensus, not compromise, but conviction, action, persistence, until the job is well and truly finished.' And economic recovery? The Prime Minister said, 'We are looking for self-starters. We are looking for princes of industry, people who have fantastic ability to build things and create jobs'. The unrealism of Thatcherism may be most perfectly expressed in this sentiment, one which rejects the state-led investment of Gaullism. Instead, we are offered an authoritarian populism, a celebrant militarism, a pitiful nostalgia, the export of capital, fewer jobs for lower real wages, non-existent 'princes of industry', and, oh yes, the Falklands.

5 Pastoralism and Expatriotism

WHAT WAS THE nature of the support for the Falklands war in Britain? Was the kingdom really as united behind the task force as the media suggested? Hopefully, studies will appear that will allow a tight answer to this question. At present we may only speculate.* But I would suggest that while there was overwhelming endorsement of the expedition rather than hostility towards it, the depth and character of popular support varied. To a considerable degree it was not much more than passive assent. This is not said to diminish the gravity of majority support for the war, which certainly existed, but it should be distinguished from the hoopla of the Tories. Enthusiasm for the fighting was not as strong as identification with the troops. Many who wanted them to win once they landed on the islands—and hence thought something 'worth' fighting for—did not relish the defeat of Argentina with Thatcher's gusto. For example, on 25 April, a British advance force recaptured South Georgia, a dependency 800 miles from the Falklands which Argentina had seized with a small force. Thatcher appeared on prime TV news to announce the victory. She called upon her compatriots to 'rejoice'. But few did. Similarly, the headlines were larger than their readers' emotions.

Questions about the kind of support that the Armada garnered suggest themselves along lines of region, class and gender. Within the UK it seemed that backing for the war was stronger in England than in Scotland or Wales, in intensity if not in numbers. English nationalism appears to take the form of Great Britishness: The cross of St George does not have enough colour in it for the English, and they need a larger geographical entity than their own nation. This may be most obvious in England's attachment to Northern Ireland, but the attitude emerged sharply during the Falklands war. For Thatcher especially, a *united* Kingdom means an expansionist assertion of nationalism, revealed by her claim that she had put the 'Great' back into Britain. This feeling is more prevalent in England, which has still to accept its small country status, than in Wales or Scotland. While many Scots and Welsh feel a dual allegiance (even if they feel that they are British first and then Scottish or Welsh), most English will be puzzled if not confounded by the question of identity. For them it is not a dual affiliation: they are both English and British, the latter is really the global expression of the former and completely 'natural' to it. The more their Englishness comes into question, however, as it did with the *English* riots of 1981, the more many will welcome an assertion of their Great Britishness. The Falklands episode may not be the last of such demonstrations, even if it remains the clearest. Yet we can be sure that 'Great Britishness' will pass away eventually for it is a claim upon the world and the world has now moved on.

There seemed to be no class divisions over the Falklands. Support was not only widespread, it cut across political and social divisions. Or did it? Even after a brilliantly executed and cleverly publicized military victory, twenty per cent of the population expressed opposition to the war.[1] In overall party terms there was a landslide in favour of the expedition. Nonetheless, one person in five came out against it even when it succeeded, which on consideration seems rather surprising. The press nowhere reflected this kind of hostility to Thatcher's adventure.[2] The most eloquent expression of disgust at the majority approval came, perhaps, from John Fowles. The public do not, or cannot stop murder, he wrote, 'because they are hog-tied by false assumptions, by apathy, by tradition, by social myth and convention, by inability to think before words like "honour", "duty", "pride" and the rest.'[3] Against this, Tony Benn has asserted that opposition to the fighting became so considerable that he is not persuaded that the public really supported the war. Another of Benn's points is more convincing, when he argues, 'war agitates people in the sense of making them think. There was a lot more serious discussion in those ten weeks than the media allowed us to know about ...'.[4]

Those who identify with the ruling institutions of Britain, expressed a class fervour in their support for Thatcher. They knew that their position domestically would be strengthened and, indeed, that this was what the battle was really about, as this was where 'humiliation' and 'confidence' came home to roost. On the other hand, much of the working class and pub support for the fighting was a 'non-political' endorsement of the war. Mass patriotism represents itself as, and is felt to be, 'above' or 'aside' from politics, especially in the party sense. It draws upon the individual's desire for a cause, for courage, excitement and vicarious risk. Many in Britain are tired of politics, they resent the interminable difficulties and frustrations of party manifestos and economic programmes. The war allowed them to get away from the erosion of morale induced by decline, unemployment and complexities.

Also, perhaps, when people have lost their own nerve and are scared, they like to support those who are daring and take risks. The Falklands was a classic instance of the intimidated identifying with their intimidator, as others became the victims. On a larger scale, although most people in Britain do not believe in imperial structures any longer, at least to the extent that they are unwilling to lay down their lives for them, they are nonetheless frightened at the prospect of their disappearance.

Thus the British expedition to the Falklands gathered support in all sorts of ways and drew on a strange combination of historic folk-memories. Yet its obviously ludicrous objective, a far-away pimple, was hardly worthy of such passions and the sacrifice of young lives, and many felt that too. The Mitcham and Morden by-election took place on 3 June as British forces were moving towards victory at Port Stanley. The Conservatives won; only three months before this might have seemed inconceivable. Yet in what was a crucial and much publicised electoral event, half of the voters stayed at home. That does not mean that they opposed the war, but it might mean a considerable degree of unease over the way it was being used. At any rate even *The Times* was obliged to agree that public support was subdued. At the beginning (as we will see) it projected its own fervour onto the British masses, and thought there might be a need to restrain 'public hysteria' and stop the mob from 'burning effigies'. At the end of the war it noted instead that while 'the spirit of Britain has been rediscovered ... it came to individuals not the mass. There were no mass rallies, no shouting, no parades.'[5] Indeed, when Thatcher left No 10 Downing Street to go and make her victory statement to the House of Commons, the *Guardian* reported,

> By all accounts yesterday should have been a red letter day in British history. Yet the small, subdued crowd in Whitehall and Downing Street gave little indication that the crisis in the Falklands was over. Even at its peak, the crowd swelled to no more than 200 as the triumphant Margaret Thatcher emerged ...[6]

In addition there was evidence that opposition to the British expedition was gathering strength. Anti-war demonstrations, although small, were larger than any pro-war mobilizations. The Easter CND rally in central London was massive and properly hostile to the Falklands war. Furthermore, as Thatcher's desire for a military confrontation became more obvious, the initial 'innocence' of the British position gave way to a more accurate picture. There was indeed some kind of learning process underway and if Britain had become bogged down in a protracted engagement in the Falklands, a serious anti-war movement would certainly have developed.

It seems to me, therefore, that while Benn is, if anything, far too complacent about 'public opinion', Fowles is over pessimistic in his formulation. There was massive support for the war, but it was relatively restrained and much more open to argument than the caricature of unredeemed jingoist sentiment. When a service was held at St Paul's to commemorate the dead, Thatcher and her accolytes were said to be furious that the Church had successfully stifled any rejoicing at the victory. They wanted instead a triumphalist note to reinforce and legitimize Thatcher's claims that Britain had proved itself to be once more the country that ruled a quarter of the world. But the absence of this theme did not disturb the families bereaved by the conflict. Indeed, the strident warmongers seemed to be isolated in their outburst and the Church of England's restraint was justified in popular terms. Thus while Fowles's denunciation of public apathy, of tradition and myth is particularly welcome, these attributes did not show themselves to be unassailable or unalterable. Labour's shambolic patriotic opportunism may make its leaders desire to sweep the whole episode under the carpet. But those who were against the war, or even its more primitive manifestations, will do well to keep the issue and arguments alive, and to challenge, as Fowles himself has done, the definition of country and virtue that Parliament has prescribed.

The right-wing will doubtless give its assent to the demand that there be 'No more Falklands', but will interpret this to mean that there should be a *larger* Navy so as to 'deter' any future aggression, there and elsewhere. In fact it is obvious that those who enjoyed the war will want another like it: a conflict that they can contain and win. In strategic terms, the issue hinges on the Royal Navy. There can be little doubt that if there was one organized and effective lobby which pushed for the war and lined up MPs in its support, it was the Navy lobby rather than the Falklands Association. In its view, the war has proved the need for aircraft carriers and a trans-global maritime strike force. Since the hard-fought decision to abolish carriers, taken in 1966, the Navy has dragged out their existence and pushed through the construction of spuriously designated 'through-deck cruisers' like the *Invincible*, which went into commission in 1980 at a cost of £250 million. As James Bellini argued prior to the Falklands episode, the Navy building programme has been a classic example of an entrenched military bureaucracy frustrating political decisions.[7]

There was once a time, during the idealistic high tide of the new left, when it was argued that the proletariat would reach its self-emancipation only when it became properly a conscious class that was fully 'for-itself'. Whether or not this was ever a suitable ambition for the working class, the Royal Navy has beaten them to it. Today, the British navy is indeed a fleet that exists to express the glory of its own self-conscious existence. The Falklands, population at most 1,800, has proved the 'need' for a force of more than 70,000.

Each capital ship 'needs' a flotilla of support vessels to service and protect it. They in turn 'need' supply and fuel ships to keep them going, in the empty, fathomless sea, to ensure them against attack. The imperial, South Atlantic role of the Royal Navy has no strategic purpose in terms of balance of power—there are no other powers there. It diminishes rather than assists the commercial interests of the United Kingdom. But, if it was not there, would Britain then lose another Falklands war? No, this would merely ensure that there would not *be* a second Falklands war. The Navy is there, quite simply, for itself.

Another aspect of support for the fighting which was perhaps much-joked about but not taken seriously, was the role of women. To what extent did women and men endorse or oppose the expedition in different ways? The question quickly shifted onto the aura of Margaret Thatcher herself. In an editorial in their August issue, the *Spare Rib* collective denounced the 'idiotic and irresponsible patriotic fervour' of the war and suggested it was an expression of 'male power'.[8] White middle class women who climbed the existing ladder, it continued, tend to reinforce this culture, just as Thatcher has done, rather than combat its domination. Meanwhile Thatcher herself explains her own supremacy through received stereotypes of the woman's role. In her post-victory interview granted to the *Daily Express*, she told George Gale of her fears,

I had the winter at the back of my mind. *The winter*. What will the winter do? The wind, the cold. Down in South Georgia the ice, what will it do? It beat Napoleon at Moscow.[9]

But when Gale asked her whether being a woman made any difference, Thatcher immediately domesticated her Napoleonic obsession with the Falklands, which she admitted 'became my life, it became my bloodstream'. Instead, 'it may just be', she put it, feigning homeliness,

that many, many women make naturally good managers. You might not think of it that way, George, but each woman who runs a house is a manager and an organizer. We thought forward each day, and we did it in a routine way, and we were on the job 24 hours a day.

In Thatcher's view, while men talk, women act. As she presents it her emergence at the helm of the Tory Party is not at all an exceptional achievement. Rather, in a Party of blatherers and windbags, she with her active duster and clear sense of the domestic economy and its priorities, 'gets on with the job' and sees it through. She is the matriarch of an iron home.

In fact, I think it is clear that Thatcher's womanhood has been crucial to her success so far, even though why this is so remains an open question. It is one that is difficult to address beyond the sniggers which it induces. Yet without her feminine sincerity, would Thatcher have gained the leadership of the Conservative Party? For a start it allowed her to mean what she said without being taken seriously. Take, for example, Thatcher's love of guns and weapons, and her oft expressed admiration for Britain's 'marvellous' fighting men. Such sentiments advocated by a man would seem to be either the projections of a camp gay or those of an unhinged fanatic. Being a woman allowed Thatcher to combine both elements and thus domesticate Powellism.

But however domesticated, the stridency of Thatcher's nationalism is abnormal for a Prime Minister. Many in the British upper classes found it rather foreign, as the St Paul's service showed. It was not the deployment of the fleet they found disturbing, but Thatcher's evident *desire* for a purifying conflict, her adamantine rejection of reasonable compromise, the strutting insistence upon global 'principles', that appeared 'un-British'. Those with experience knew perfectly well that all the talk about 'self-determination' was so much prattle, even when they shared a feeling of national humiliation, and wanted to rectify the country's 'honour'. It was a splendid risk to send the Armada and a great relief when the troops were put ashore so triumphantly. British skill had been demonstrated and pride had been restored in the old lion. But then it was time to settle rather than press on and commit the UK to a conflict with Argentina in perpetuity. There was and is nothing 'wet' about such an attitude, which is realistic and practical. Earlier, I noted how the fight for the Falklands seems incongruous when compared to Britain's handover of territories many times its own size all around the world. Thatcher has sought to reverse this constitutive aspect of imperial pragmatism, just as she has massively exacerbated unemployment and challenged the state's commitment to social security. Her use of Churchillian rhetoric to assault the legacy of Churchillism has even led her to defy Washington, which is sure to try and repair its relations with Agentina. Suppose when the next US administration comes into office in two years time, it has garnered the considerable Hispanic votes in such key states as New York and California and so is pledged to a more hemispheric orientation. The Falklands never sat comfortably with the Monroe doctrine; it would be folly for Britain to cross America because of them. Firmness and resolution today have to be tempered by policies which allow for the imperatives of tomorrow.

All this seems obvious enough, so how was Thatcher able to defy the post-war traditions of Britain in the name of old England with such ease? In truth, 'Britain' is oddly uncomfortable in its own skin. How many countries is the United Kingdom? Can the British be nationalists when the word 'nationalism' applied to the UK only recently meant the activities of extremist groups in the Celtic fringe? Can the ordinary 'Briton' be loyal to both Europe and the Queen? The stuttered self-correction by Sir Bernard Braine, should not be forgotten: is it the blood of the *English* that boils especially fast? And if so, what has happened to that national trait for which the English pride themselves across the world, *sangfroid*? How can the self-composure of the gentleman and the dry tenacity of the working man, whose combination in officers and other ranks constitutes the national image of the British army, be represented by a newspaper (the *Sun*) that headlines GOTCHA! when the *Belgrano* is sunk with over 300 dead?

When Dr Johnson wrote his pamphlet on the Falklands in 1770 he assailed those who wanted war with Spain over the islands. 'Patriotism is the last refuge of a scoundrel', he declared. The word 'patriot' had a more radical sense at that time then it does today, and Johnson was arguing on behalf of the government who paid him. The word now tends to mean love of one's country, in a beneficent way, but in the UK it shades rapidly into an assertion of historic domination overseas and a valorization of the special kinds of class rule Britain suffers at home.

Take, for example, a widespread English response to the Junta's seizure of the Falklands: 'We cannot allow ourselves to be bullied'. Many supported the Armada with this sentiment. A worker uses the collective pronoun 'we', which belongs in its full sense to the sovereign class and those who consciously identify with it. The worker extends it not only to him- (or her-) self, a member of a class with quite different interests, but also to 'the country as a whole', something that all classes do indeed share in their antagonistic way. But then, in addition, the 'we' is stretched 8,000 miles to territory none had spared a thought for until that moment. And this was an instinctive reaction for many. It was not merely a passive response to the Parliamentary debate, a kind of docking of the forelock to the wisdom of MPs! Nor, either, was the feeling the result of instant manipulation by the press and television although that helped. Rather, the reaction stemmed from inherited presumptions momentarily and vividly encouraged. Was the attitude thus expressed one of *patriotism*—the defence of a common identity from aggression? Or was it *nationalism*—the assertion of one's country's greatness compared to others? Or was it *imperialism*—the imposition of national dominance overseas?

It was all these three things at once: a specifically British amalgamation, that stems from a peculiar, defensive articulation of

England's global role. In the nineteenth century as the world's foremost power it carried the burden of civilization to darker, 'more excitable' parts, did it not? To be dominant in so many places meant being almost always under attack. That was part of the 'burden', the heavy duty that accompanied keeping the peace. At the same time, although Britain ruled the waves it did not rule Europe. It called its Empire the *Pax Britannica*, the Latin suggested that London was the new Rome. Yet this world power, far greater in extent and population than the Roman Empire at its height, never established direct control over continental Europe. The actual boundaries of the Roman Empire were outside London's grasp except for England itself. The British Empire was a Third World one whose home country remained vulnerable to the re-creation of a 'Roman' Empire in Europe whether by Napoleonic France or Nazi Germany. An element of self-defence remained a powerful component of British imperialism, not so much because its outposts were attacked or its natives 'mutinied', but because between what was 'ours' out there and here at home lay 'the continent', always threatening to come between us and our possessions. Even worse, a forceful, united Europe would inevitably lay claim to England and reduce it 'once more' to the subaltern outpost it was at the time of Rome. Finally, in the last years of the Empire itself, just before it became dust, fact and fancy merged as a Europe unified by Fascism really did pose a direct threat to Britain. In response, Churchillism recuperated the loyalty of all strata in an amalgam that fused together patriotic defence of country and belief in empire through a defiant, nationalist anti-fascism.

To resurrect this Churchillian patriotism now is indeed the action of scoundrels, except that the word is too archaic to carry sufficient opprobrium. Britain itself is not under attack or threat of invasion. It no longer has an Empire to 'defend'. The themes of Churchillism have been tapped, but for quite other purposes than those for which it was created. The way that Thatcher has usurped the ideals of World War Two has been as obnoxious as the way Michael Foot served them up to her on a plate. It has brought dishonour to the war against Fascism, to see it compared to the Falklands dispute. Ever since 1945, the political Right has attempted to wrest all the credit for the popular mobilization of 1940, in which the Left and liberals played, as we have seen, a decisive part. It has been tragic and pathetic for socialists to witness the trust with which Labour finally capitulated, and handed over that wartime legacy to Thatcherism. There was not a word from the opposition front bench that the price of patriotism in 1940 was full employment. Should it be sold cheaper now? 'Yes', was the unanimous reply of the enfeebled successors of Attlee; who was hardly more than a mouse from all accounts but who presumably would have known better than to have entrusted a Conservative Cabinet to preserve the 'way of life' of 1,800 people with an Armada, when the same Tories were destroying the way of life of millions just down the road.

In 1949 Michael Foot co-authored a booklet that was, in effect, an election screed for Labour. It condemned the Conservatives for their record in the 1930s and was titled, *Who Are The Patriots?* Today we know the answer. Dr Johnson's phrase has rolled through two centuries to find its triumphant justification in the House of Commons. Yet something had changed. There was no need for the war-party to clamour for a fight over the Falklands in 1982. Even to suggest reluctance over the dangers of the conflict was sufficient to be howled down and have charges of 'traitor' levelled against one. It was those who were not scoundrels who were in need of refuge, as a torrent of patriotic hyperbole was unleashed.

For Parliament did not stand alone when it called for war. On the contrary, the peculiarly 'un-British' sentiments of the House and the Prime Minister were kept up to the mark by a continuous invective from the press. In particular, the pace was set by the Australian-owned stable of newspapers controlled by Rupert Murdoch. He had made his first beach-head with the *News of the World*, (a Sunday paper that on April 25 headlined one editorial, WHY WE MUST GO TO WAR). Murdoch had gone on to capture the *Sun* (a paper for the lumpen) and *The Times*. The latter two together conducted a daily pincer movement on opinion. They were only a part of the media chorus yet they both managed to do something new in terms of nationalist extremism, and they may signal the future direction of English 'patriotism'. Certainly they reinforced the novel, inflexible nationalist element in Thatcherism. While others will doubtless provide an overall examination of the media coverage on the Falklands, here only the contribution of the two Murdoch dailies will be discussed.

Who would wish to suggest that their dual approach was co-ordinated? Each editorial commander surely took all the tactical decisions according to his own lights. After all, although both the *Sun* and *The Times* have the same owner, he might be many thousands of miles away. Yet it is difficult not to consider that the very 'distance' of Murdoch from Britain contributed to the hysterical artifice displayed by both papers. The *Sun* ran as a daily slogan from its masthead 'The Paper That Supports Our Boys'. It was not just that it seemed to cash in on the war for circulation purposes; it struck the posture of someone who needed to prove his nationalism by extra zealotry. Similarly, *The Times* was so overcome by Churchillism that it took the analogy with the Second World War *literally*. Twice its editorials compared the fight for the

Falklands with the declaration of war over Poland in 1939. (It took Neal Ascherson to point out, 'If Britain stands by the Falklands as she stood by Poland in 1939, a fifth of the islanders will die, Port Stanley will be razed and the islanders will end up under the hegemony of a foreign power.'[10])

Preposterous, flag-waving insistence that only the zealous are real patriots and that those who do not agree are 'traitors', a fixation on past battles as if they are being fought-out still at this very moment, have been frequently observed in the United Kingdom – in Ulster. It is not without reason that those *removed* from England, yet feeling the necessity to be attached to it, become the most vociferous nationalists. Already a Thatcherite and under attack for the cavalier treatment of his editors, Murdoch would have been less than human if he had not felt any need to *prove* the loyalty of his papers to the nation. Global corporations are always inclined to pay the local Ceasar in national currency; it is a corporate form of attachment and insurance. Both for settlers removed from the 'mother' country—from Ulster and Gibraltar to the Kelpers themselves—and also for antipodean proprietors of organs of opinion, perhaps we should call this intense yet dislocated national sentiment *expatriotism*. At any rate, international tit-and-bum-capitalism rose to the occasion.

For *The Times*, an ageing pensioner, it was primarily a matter of emotions and inaccuracy. It stated in its massive editorial of April 5, 'Emotion is no sound basis for successful strategic thinking'. It is always a danger sign when such a proviso is made; only those in the grip of emotion feel the need to reassure themselves that they are 'cool'. So, having strived to gain control of its senses, *The Times* continued:

> There can be—there must be—no doubt about our strategic objective. As the Prime Minister said in the Commons on Saturday, the Falkland Islands are British territory, inhabited by British citizens. They have been invaded by enemy forces. Those forces must be removed. The authority of Britain must be reasserted over the Islands.

There can be, there must be ... The Prime Minister did not—no she did not—say that the Falklands are inhabited by British citizens. She said that they 'are British in stock', 'British in allegiance', but not citizens, for her own administration had denied them that title less than two years before, in its Nationality Act. The same editorial emphasized that 'we must have the wisdom to identify' our 'political objectives', 'if we are to prevail'. Wisdom as distinct from emotion. Once one has declared oneself wise, who would be so small minded as to carp about inaccuracies when what mattered was the heart of strategy:

> As in 1939, so today; the same principles apply to the Falklands. We have given our word, and we must, where we can, prevent the expansionist policies of a dictatorship affecting our interests. But there is a more important dimension now. The Poles were Poles; the Falklanders are our people. They are British citizens. The Falkland Islands are British territory. When British territory is invaded, it is not just an invasion of our land, but of our whole spirit. We are all Falklanders now.

And so the editorial, spread over most of an entire page, was called, WE ARE ALL FALKLANDERS NOW. We can leave aside the fact that the Falkland Islands are not 'our land', in the sense that no one who conjures up the word 'Britain' imagines the Falklands to be included. (This is not a question of their small size and distance, one can now think of America as including Hawaii.) All that one needs to do is to re-write this supposed zenith of strategic thinking in a way that is factually accurate for its atmospheric assertions to collapse. For example,

> But there is a more important dimension now. The Poles were Poles but the Falklanders are our people. Two years ago we denied them British citizenship. Nonetheless ....

It does not work. And for a highly entertaining reason. Racialism. The same racialist rejection of nationality rights for the Falkland Islanders (basicly because of the example it might set for Hong Kong[11]) also lies behind the attitude of *The Times* editorial; how else is one to explain the suggestion that 1,800 of 'our people' are 'more important' than the fate of Poland on the brink of the Second World War? Indeed, this is how the editorial waxed in its penultimate section:

> The national will to defend itself has to be cherished and be replenished if it is to mean something real in a dangerous and unpredictable world. Mr Enoch Powell told the Commons that the next few weeks would see whether the 'Iron Lady' was truly of that metal. It is not just a time to test her resolve but that of all the British people.
>   We are an island race, and the focus of attack is one of our islands, inhabited by our islanders.

The elision between the people who live on the Falklands and London's sovereign pride could hardly be more evident. The way the two are intermingled here is drawn from the Parliamentary debate and given a final stamp. The islanders are pressed into the opportunity to 'replenish' the 'national will'. What matters is not their lives but that the islanders themselves are us and *ours*: part of our 'Island Race'.

The Times recognized that, 'There may have to be a fight about-it, in which people will get hurt.' Given its analogy with World War Two, this was a decent admission. The whole piece, then, was wierdly unbalanced. On 20 May another, particularly astonishing example of its disturbance appeared, headed, THE STILL SMALL VOICE OF TRUTH. This was a reference by *The Times* to itself. Parliament should return to 'simplicity' at the 'sombre' moment when it was going to debate the Falklands crisis for the last time before the by then inevitable escalation to full scale ground attack. How should this be done?

> An individual becomes more complete within himself by a conscious act of understanding the forces of disorder which rage within him, and by reference to some constant source of morality, an evaluation of the immense power of evil in the world, and the fact that mankind as a whole – nations, societies, and groups – are all capable of becoming merely instruments of that evil, is part of that understanding; and part of that morality.

What raging force lay behind the composition of this sentence?

One hesitates to consider its psychopathology and rather dismisses such nonsense as the result of a hangover. Yet there is something important here, that is being tapped and exploited by a newspaper that has just helped to lead a country into war. The idea of evil and good—of right and wrong at a deeper level than correct behaviour—is profoundly important. Without it we cannot judge wars: when to fight in them and when not. But to write about evil today, it is necessary to remove the notion from its religious context and to give it a non-mystical existence in the relations between people. Ironically, it is in many cases priests who have pioneered this secularization. (They are not embarrassed by the vocabulary and many of those who work in the Third World especially have rejected the repressive role of the Church.) Of course, I am not suggesting that *The Times* be taken seriously on the subject of evil; the notion needs to be rescued from the clammy hands of its leader writers. Their fundamental incapacity when confronted with the issue is evident in their attempt to utilize it for an improper purpose. One way of spotting when such things occur is the endless repetition of the word, like some incantation. Thus the 20 May editorial in *The Times* opened with a statement that Argentina's aggression was 'an evil thing'. A united Britain, the paper claimed, had apparently recognized that the invasion of the Falklands—in which it should be recalled the invaders took no lives—was,

> an incontrovertably *evil* act. Obviously there have been disagreements

about the methods of coping with that *evil*, but there should be recognition that to compromise with *evil*—to appease it—is to run the risk of having to share responsibility for it. How we react to *evil* must therefore be conditioned by the need to compromise with it as little as possible, while taking care to see that our reaction to it does not compound the original *evil*. Parliament will today again discuss the affair. (My emphasis.)

What then of the killings and maimings that will follow? *The Times*, true to its demand for unemotional weighing of strategy, would not duck the issue. 'There may be *unpleasantness* in the course of that combat, which can only be endured with a vision of some greater good beyond it.' (My emphasis.)

What is the 'greater good' beyond the battlefield and its 'unpleasantness'? What is it *really* that the British are fighting for, when they seek to 'replenish' their national character? By a stroke of good fortune, the day of the 20 May editorial was also the day after Winchester, the doyen of Public Schools, celebrated its 600th anniversary. This too was the subject of a *Times* editorial. It came just below the 'Still Small Voice of Truth' (see illustration). 'We honour Winchester today for its hardened and shameless elitism ... you could say that government ministers are Old Etonians, their permanent secretaries are Old Wykehamists.' Could *this* be what 'we' are fighting for? Is such an arrangement to be the perpetual reality of 'self-determination' in Britain, that Ministers are schooled at Eton while policy is controlled by those who have been to Winchester?

It would be optimistic perhaps to suggest that Winchester has now entered its final century. Yet the evidence of *The Times* itself, and its tremulous repetition of 'evil' points to a terminal decline however slow. Imagine, for example, that one is canvassing for votes or opinions and one meets an old lady. She is evidently an Irish Catholic who lives by herself. There is a good chance that she too will start telling you about evil. Hers, she may tell you, is only a 'still small voice'. There are so many 'evil things' about, so much 'power of evil', so much need to 'combat evil', she too is likely to say, with utter conviction. Perhaps she really has been mugged, or some ruthless landlord from the antipodes has just taken over her premises and is evicting life-long tenants, and what could be more evil than that? It would be tasteless to argue with the old lady. How she feels is quite understandable as she slips, lonely and insecure, into her final years.

The moment of dying nerve can hardly have gone down well with the landlord. The *Sun* outshone *The Times*, it may be said, even though they were celestial twins. Whenever a country goes to war, it will often disclaim its actual aims. The statements of the great

THE STILL SMALL VOICE OF TRUTH

Since the invasion of the Falklands on April 2, there has been the sound of many voices. Yet at the heart of the matter, it was an evil thing, an injustice, an aggression. Nobody disputes that. Even loyal Argentines — let alone Argentina's apologists — accept that force should not have been used to prosecute the Argentine case. But force was used; and it was not necessary. Beneath the roll of Argentine drums there are voices, however small, however still, which say that too, and they recognize that the unity achieved by the junta in Buenos Aires may only be a passing one, since it was born of an injustice. Unity in Britain, on the other hand, is based on recognition of the invasion as an incontrovertibly evil act. Obviously there have been disagreemnents about the method of coping with that evil, but there should be recognition that to compromise with evil — to appease it — is to run the risk of having to share responsibility for it. How we react to evil must therefore be conditioned by the need to compro mise with it as little as possil.'e, while taking care to see that our reaction to it does not compound the original evil.

Parliament will today again discuss the affair. It is a sombre moment. Amid all the tumult and the argument it would do well to return to simplicity; and to search for that still, small voice of truth which recognises the basic injustice of what occurred. Recognition of that fact is the first stage of reflection. Reflection should precede reaction. The world is full of confusion and disorder, which is repeated both among societies and within the minds of individuals.

There is a lack of orientation, and a consequent searching for symbols of order and constancy. An individual becomes more complete within himself by a conscious act of understanding the forces of disorder which rage within him, and by reference to some constant source of morality, an evaluation of the immense power of evil in the world, and the fact that mankind as a whole — nations, societies and groups — are all capable of becoming merely instruments of that evil, is part of that understanding; and part of that morality.

By all accounts the British Government has made compromises in the course of a peaceful solution, but not ones which invalidate the ultimate threat to use force to undo the original aggression. If force has to be used, it is well to temper it with recognition of the need to search for some greater good to come out of a moment of evil. So Parliament has the opportunity again today to reflect the unity which the nation has shown on this single and paramount point of recognising an injustice. In their different ways British people have united round the necessity to combat injustice and not to concede to it. There may be unpleasantness in the course of that combat, which can only be endured with a vision of some greater good beyond it.

We are at a moment of choice. It is quite a simple one, really. Parliament, on our behalf on April 3, chose to combat evil; it must therefore live with the consequences, but see that it can mould those consequences into further choices. Morality — individual, social, national, indeed the morality of all mankind — is about choice. There can be no choice without the freedom — the hard won freedom — to choose. That is the still, small voice which should be heard above the parliamentary hubbub today.

THE SHAMELESS ELITE

It is right and proper that the Queen visited the Grammar School of the College of the Blessed Mary of Winchestre by Winchestre to honour the six hundredth anniversary of its foundation yesterday: not because it is part of Her invisible Establishment, though it is; not because she favours private over state education, though she does, at any rate in choice of schools for her own children; and not because Winchester set the pattern for Henry VI's foundation at Eton College, and all other arriviste, Johnny-come-later public schools, though it did.

It is right because for six centuries Winchester has given the most intellectually excellent education available to "poor and indigent" scholars, as well as subsequently to others less indigent, whose parents could recognize a good education when they saw one. For a country to be able to boast one of the oldest and greatest schools in the world is no small thing. We are rightly proud of the roots of our English culture, and Winchester is one of the deepest.

We honour Winchester today for its hardened and shameless elitism, in the good sense of that vexatious and controversial word. Elitism is a boo-word in our egalitarian age. But if it means preferring the best to the second-rate in the world of ideas it is still a virtue. This is not the place, for there is not room, to go into the vexed question of William of Wykeham's motto for his educational foundations. Manners have been interpreted to mean anything from style to exaggerated punctilio. Wykehamists are not noted for their good manners in the modern sense of opening doors for women. Today's women would not thank them, anyway. The defining characteristic anecdote has a Wykehamist, an Etonian, and a Harrovian in a room when a lady comes in. The Wykehamist calls out for somebody to fetch a chair. The Etonian goes and gets one. And the Harrovian sits down in it himself.

What Wykehamists are conspicuous for is not manners in the modern sense of courtesy, but intellectual superiority, which can tilt into snobbery. They look at you not as though you are improperly dressed, though you may be, but as though you have just committed a solecism or forgotten a line of Shakespeare's eighteenth sonnet. If you wanted to be critical, you could say that the school overemphasizes analytic intelligence at the expense of creativity. If you wanted to be trite, you could say that while government ministers are Old Etonians, their permanent secretaries are Old Wykehamists. If you wanted to be wet, you could say that it is cruel to expose children of tender years to the horrors of parsing the Latin words *potato* and *beer*. If you wanted to be fair and truthful on the old place's six hundredth anniversary, you could borrow the words from a school with better songs and say *Floreat, florebit*.

Editorials in THE TIMES, 20 May 1982

powers especially should always be read in their opposite form, to help fill out the picture: that which they denounce, they may well be about to commit. So too with the Murdoch empire. *The Times* of 5 April sent out the instruction:

> There must be no nonsense of burning effiges, irrelevant spite or public hysteria. The public imagination can so quickly and so easily be gripped by propaganda which can only distort and aggravate the issue.

The statement should be read as incitement as much as warning: The public *can* be easily gripped by propaganda, in that respect 'we' are still its masters. The *Sun*, whose task is precisely to grip the public imagination on as wide a scale as possible, got to work.

It cashed in on the pornography of missiles. It dehumanized both British and Argentinian soldiers just as it dehumanizes women: PARAS WADE INTO ARGIES was the celebration on one front page, in two-inch letters (28 May). It accused the *Daily Mirror* of 'treason' for not expressing joy at the whole affair. The *Mirror* replied with a demonstration of factual inaccuracy in the *Sun*'s reporting. Keith Waterhouse, a *Mirror* columnist, tried to finesse Dr Johnson. Some people, he said, had, 'hoisted their skull and crossbones over the English dictionary and laid claim to the word PATRIOTISM. Until this etymological junta commenced to exercise its squatting rights a patriot was one who loved his country'.[12] But as we have suggested, 'patriotism' was never as easy as that: it was always open to being usurped by those who wanted a *Great* Britain in world terms. Similarly, the *Mirror* responded with a splendid editorial that said the Murdoch paper had fallen from the gutter into the sewer. Yet even this, like Keith Waterhouse's, was a defensive response. The *Sun* was able to take the initiative. The paper to its left had no equivalent language with which it could assert in its own time and energy, the more realistic nationalism it seemed to desire.

Why was this? In part because expatriotism, while it usurps and exploits the old sentiments in its red-neck fashion, even to the point of caricature, nonetheless appeals to the 'real thing'. That is why disagreement, however trenchant, must reassess past as well as present, to succeed. Here I will only discuss two historic themes, pastoralism and heroism as they were reprocessed by the Falklands.

When Argentina seized the Falklands, film was shown on British television of recent interviews with the islanders. Their evident British accents and rural gait made a deep impression. It was as if 'the Nazis had taken over the Archers'.[13] Again, the reference might seem opaque to foreigners. *The Archers* is 'an everyday story of countryfolk', broadcast daily since 1951 from the small fictitious village of 'Ambridge'. 'There is some corner in the English mind that is forever Ambridge', noted one observer, who added 'rightly or wrongly, the village represents an ideal living state'.[14] The ideal of the countryside and 'countryfolk' is an immensely powerful cultural force not only in England, but in Scotland and Wales as well. Martin Wiener has provided an extensive documentation of the ubiquity and the centrality of rural ideals in British political and economic life. From the mid-nineteenth century to the present, and especially from Baldwin's 'England is the country', to Callaghan's acquisition of a farm from whose gate he was photographed, Baldwin-like, as Prime Minister (it provides a link with 'the peasant in us', commented Mrs Callaghan); Wiener shows that rusticity holds both Right and Left in a joint condemnation of 'industrialism'.

It is easy to be scathing about the country-cottage fetish and allotment consciousness of the English, which, with its strain of retreat, determination against the rain and self-sufficiency, was one of the binding subseams of Churchillism. The suture of interclass, capitalist hegemony has been hand-sewn with a rural stitch in England, to give it added strength. At the same time, as Wiener points out, the country was 'available for use as an integrating cultural symbol' precisely because it was virtually empty and hence safe. 'The vision of a tranquilly rustic and traditional national way of life (which) permeated English life' originated with massive depopulation of the actual countryside.[15] Vacant land is sacred.

This reflection might seem of slight relevance to an analysis of the Falklands Crisis; in fact, it helps explain the strange social empathy with such a distant corner of the world. The joining together of support for the Armada from distinct, and even antagonistic, sectors of the population was partially shaped by shared, historic attitudes of nostalgia towards an 'empty' countryside, at once as remote and as mythologically intimate as Ambridge. By contrast, had the population of the islands been engaged in a company mineworks, the evidently industrial nature of their settlement might not have been so accommodating to mythologization—and a generous, negotiated compromise might not have seemed 'inhuman' or destructive of the local 'British way of life'. Ironically it was the very blighted quality of the rural setting that made the Falklanders seem so 'organic' and 'noble'. The English consciousness with its gentrified repression of urban and industrial reality regards the tiny village as somehow central and the towns—in which 90 per cent of the population lives—as artificial. The solitary life of the Kelpers seemed to have had a kind of ultimate authenticity.

Furthermore, the allure of rural imagery in a (bitterly) ironic military setting, also has a notable tradition which dates back to the formative shock of the Great War and its trenches. In his exceptionally revealing cultural history, Paul Fussell shows how the intense ruralism of English culture (he notes that half the poems in the *Oxford Book of English Verse* are about flowers) was turned to a new use in the literary response to the 1914-18 conflict. 'Recourse to the pastoral is an English mode of both fully gauging the calamities of the Great War and imaginatively protecting oneself against them.'[16] Reading his book after the Falklands War, one cannot help but be struck by the ludicrous descent of media cant from the first full experience of modern war that Britain underwent. A minor irony is the Island's sheep, an image consistently used about the men who went obediently to their slaughter after 1914; used not just in contempt or protest but also in homoerotic compassion, as the lambs whose sacrificial blood will flow to feed the poppies.[17] In 1982 an anti-war postcard captured this echo with its slogan '600,000 Sheep Can't Be Wrong'. Another theme is the beauty of the sky, to which the English seem especially attached since their romantics, an attachment theorized by Ruskin. From the trenches, of course, the sky was always visible, if only beckoning, while all men 'stood-to' at sunrise and sunset, the moments of the heaven's magnificent intensity.[18] Again, reporters in the Falklands were always commenting upon the light and the sky. The riveting skyscapes of Vietnam and Cambodia, by contrast, never drew such breathless description from American reporters.

All these seemingly remote, arcadian notations were brought to bear, apparently naively and all the more effectively, by Lord Shackleton when he spoke about the Falklands on the day after the Argentinian invasion. Shackleton as well as being a Lord is a *Labour* peer and the son of the famous *global* explorer. As such he is one personification of mid-century Churchillism. He had been sent to the Falklands in 1975 to report on the colony, and his description of life there will be considered in Chapter 7. On 3 April 1982, he spoke on behalf of the Labour Party in the House of Lords debate, following Lord Carrington. Shackleton lamented the takeover and eulogized the Falklands. Some might say that their inhabitants are merely 'Scottish'. In fact, 'they might be Londoners as much as anyone else. They are totally British'. As for the Falkland Islands themselves,

> for those who like wild, windy places and empty spaces like the Shetlands, it is a very delightful place where the light is bright and clear. I remember talking to a man who came there from Coventry who told me how much happier he was there than when he was working on a production line.[19]

This summarizes what we can term 'Falklands Pastoralism': the windswept voids embraced by an English rural aesthetic; the stress upon the beauties of the light; the 'Britishness' affirmed, and above all the contrast, apparently powerful, actually trite, between the happiness of a blighted rural existence and the treatment humans receive on the production line. The contrast is a cheap one not only because without the line there would be no community on the Falklands today, but also because of the crass caricature of working class urbanism and even middle class suburbanism which is implied. Our pre-eminently industrial existence is reduced in living terms to the worst excesses of machine assembly.

A multiple echo can be heard in Shackleton's ruminations upon the brightness of the South Atlantic sky and the press reports of the same. For when Ruskin produced his theory of the qualities of the atmosphere, he drew upon the same metaphor as *The Times*: 'The still small voice'. It comes from I Kings 19.

> And behold, the LORD passed by, and a great and a strong wind rent the mountains, and brake in pieces the rocks before the LORD: but the LORD was not in the wind: and after the wind an earthquake: but the LORD was not in the earthquake.
> And after the earthquake a fire: but the LORD was not in the fire: and after the fire a still small voice.

In this fashion did God speak to Elijah. Today a newspaper which once prided itself on being called 'The Thunderer' now has the audacity to claim to be the vehicle for the deity Himself. Through this elitism it also lays claim to democracy. For the English version of popular rule is that only a cultivated few seem really able to appreciate what is undoubtedly best for the many. In *Modern Painters* Ruskin lauded the open sky and was far more interesting than today's *Times*. For him, nature produces in the sky 'picture after picture, glory after glory', of such beauty that it 'is quite certain it is all done for us, and intended for our perpetual pleasure (for) every man, wherever placed'. While, 'the noblest scenes of the earth can be seen and known by but a few', 'the sky is for all; as bright as it is, it is not "too bright or good for nature's daily food" '. The sky, then, in its splendid panoramas, presents a democratic vision. God, Ruskin immediately reminds his readers, 'is not in the earthquake, nor in the fire, but in the still small voice'. The Falklands may be windy, but His brightness reaches even there. Who better to appreciate this than a Labour peer and what better reason for sending the fleet than to ensure that English eyes remain there to appreciate its isolated beauties, and English accents send back their thanks, in a still small voice?

Wiener might regard Shackleton's intervention as a vindication of the major thesis of his study as he argues that there is indeed something that can be termed an industrial 'cultural revolution', and that Britain has rejected this in favour of an anti-industrial spirit, largely rural inspired, which in turn has been responsible for the decline of the UK as a manufacturing centre.[20] In other words, Wiener accepts the validity of the opposition—the dichotomy propagandized by Victorian thinkers themselves—and he does so on the simplest terms. Yet to do so at all, is surely fatal. All things being equal, who would not prefer a country house with bad drainage, no public transport and television to a look-alike terrace dwelling with bad drainage, no public transport and television. At least, during daytime, the former has a view ... No, the point is that this contrast and the choice it implies, is itself unrealistic. It is not the benefits of country air that should be criticized, but the mythology of a rural society which is held especially by those who live in towns, to compensate for their own lives. What is needed is not so much a critique of ruralism as such, for this has indeed given expression to many fine things of lasting value, but to the English way of counter-posing town and country. A way perfectly realized by Shackleton in miniature and recognized for what it is on the larger scale by Raymond Williams,

> Our powerful images of country and city have been ways of responding to a whole social development. That is why, in the end, we must not limit ourselves to their contrast but must go on to see their interrelations and through these the real shape of the underlying crisis.[21]

Here we cannot attend to the underlying crisis. But it flickered through the strange identifications that were made during the war, with its hopes, fears and even desires for a more extended solidarity. After the British victory there were various attempts to raise money for the South Atlantic Fund. One young woman from a London salon announced, in a by no means upper class accent, that her shop would hold a 'hairdressing marathon' to bring in donations. Interviewed on radio she explained that she was doing this because,

> They are out there defending us. Because although they are out there thousands of miles away, it could be us, it could be us out there.[22]

The racial identification is obvious enough—she would not have done the same for soldiers fighting for the rights of the Diego Garcians. But it is also unlikely that she would have striven to support a community of northern industrial workers who wanted to cling to their old ways. 'It could be us out there ....' It may be that she can only make that identification culturally with an 'Ambridge' brought to her across the ether, but actually there is no 'could' about it: it really is us, 'us' back here where we are, that needs to be defended.

It was not only a rural spider that spun the identification. There was also a traditional urban theme, but one made safe by appropriating it into the heroic virtues of foreign conflict. Gareth Stedman Jones has suggested that the English working class was 're-made' in the last three decades of Victorian imperialism that culminated in the relief of Mafeking and the riotous celebrations that followed this battle success in South Africa.[23] He describes the way in which the vast human agglomeration of London, a city of trade, services and small workshops—at the time the largest in the world but almost devoid of big factories—produced a new, 'Tory' working class culture, articulated by pubs and the new music halls. It was a culture consciously separate from the improving middle classes and fatalistic rather than celebrant. The 'comic stoicism' that produced Charlie Chaplin and was to be eulogized in the 1940 Blitz, came into existence at that time, along, it may be added, with most other British traditions.

But when the mediacrats joined the task force on its way to the South Atlantic, they were overwhelmed by the novelty of what they experienced. The trumpeting of old military virtues that was the achievement of sub-editors and headline writers in London and their equivalents in TV and radio presentation in the live media, was accompanied by a genuine emotion of respect for the fighting men. One of the more graphic and telling descriptions came from Patrick Bishop,

> Most of the 15 journalists on the *Canberra* began the voyage feeling mild dread at the prospect of the enforced company of so many soldiers. We ended up 'Troopie groupies' of varying degrees of intensity, loyal to our units and fluent in military slang .... At best, I patronisingly thought, the military would be amiable but boneheaded. Many of them emerged as intelligent and tolerant.[24]

Max Hastings was more up front,

> It has been an extraordinary, genuinely uplifting experience to soldier for a few weeks with the British forces. After so many years in which we have heard and said so much about British failure in so many areas of our national life, in the past few weeks I have been exposed to almost unbroken generosity, spontaneous kindness, patience, comradeship towards a common aim.
>
> Working beside men much more tired, wet, dirty, cold, hungry than oneself, I have never been grudged a drink or a cigarette or space in a bivouac or a chance to sleep in a trench.[25]

Evidently, these are not the attitudes he would find amongst his colleagues in Fleet Street. The same impression seems to have been made on Gareth Parry of the *Guardian*,

> In three months I never heard a cross word spoken, but many a helpful and humorous one.[26]

Bishop was similarly impressed,

> The soldiers showed each other remarkable loyalty and kindness ... The comfort they gave each other was almost feminine. I remember three of them soothing a man who had shrapnel in his legs, feeding him cigarettes and reassuring him that the wounds weren't as bad as they seemed.[27]

In what circles is such behaviour so remarkable as to be somehow exceptional and unexpected? Would not factory or mine workers treat each other in the same way if one of their comrades suffered an industrial accident? The navy officer who justified to Gareth Parry the decision not to grant the seamen extra pay was aware of this side of things,

> They are pretty lucky to be here in regular employment and not on the dole queue at home.[28]

This was the source of the fortitude. For a short time the mediacrats left their well paid, intensely competitive and fashionably cynical world, to live in and share a working class milieu. They discovered that the troglodites knew how to suffer and survive, that they had a sense of humour and realism and a natural solidarity. The mediacrats were moved. There *was* bravery and hardship and sacrifice on the Falklands. But is the heroism of a teenager storming Mount Tumbledown that much greater than the determination of a middle-aged man with a family trying to last out redundancy and keep his honour and self-esteem? Or, indeed, of the heroism of a man who returns to work on the line day after day? Even within the traditionally accepted universe of 'masculine' courage and 'feminine' kindliness, the qualities that uplifted Max Hastings and his cohorts came not from the Army but from the soldiers's homes. To condemn the coverage of the war, then, involves neither belittling the bravery that was displayed nor a denial of the experience which so affected the mediacrats. What was nauseating was to read in 1982, towards the end of the century of total war, descriptions of the fighting men that betrayed little if any sense that there were lessons already learnt, and to be told that everyday working class virtues had suddenly been born again, thanks to their military uniforms. If Fleet Street and the BBC were to send their reporters to *live* with strikers, say, and share their life and wages, we might hear a great deal more about spontaneous courage, kind words and generosity in adverse circumstances in Britain. Again, that is not said to idealize the working class, who are as capable of looting as the British troops on the Falklands proved themselves to be. Indeed the often reckless values of the British worker were summed up in one respect by the ASLEF train driver, who spoke to a *Financial Times* reporter with bitterness after his strike had been broken in the aftermath of the

Falklands, 'I've been a Tory all my life but no longer after this.'[29]

An equally serious aspect of the media's role was the way it was censored. The particular importance was visual rather than factual. After some of the first air engagements, a Harrier pilot described the way he fired his Sidewinder missile: it homed in on the enemy Mirage and exploded 'as advertised'. We saw only his words. During the war there were no photographs of battlefield dead. This 'treatment' was not accidental. Don McCullin, undoubtedly Britain's most famous photo-journalist, was repeatedly refused permission to cover the Falklands. A 'high ranking military officer' vetoed his going.[30] Instead, an official 'war artist' was sent; she came from the Kitson family of military fame. McCullin records what he sees as 'the sharp end'—sometimes at great risk to himself, as recently in El Salvador—and his photographs are often shocking. Ironically, their impact is diminished by context, for as a *Sunday Times* photographer his pictures usually appear in the colour supplement alongside other images of far-away places. Idyllic holiday-spots, menthylated fields, soft-lit boudoirs, all inhabited by beautiful people, project from the outlying pages a world untouched by the maimed and beyond the reach of trenches and shrapnel. The British Ministry of Defence chose to project the Falklands war as just such an advertisement: and while the fighting was taking place and support really mattered, such images as McCullin's were ruled to be incongruous.

The manipulation was found to be acceptable in part because it fitted into a long practised mode of official understatement about casualties. The less people are allowed to know what they mean in human terms, the more they will accept. Take, for example, what was probably the most craven exchange in the House of Commons during the whole conflict. It took place just after the devastating attack on the *Sir Galahad*. John Nott had told the House of Commons that he would not release the casualty figures. Richard Crawshaw of the SDP, then put the following point to him in the guise of a question:

> Can we not take comfort from the fact that up to the present time the losses, thankfully, have been much less than could possibly have been conceived when the operation was put into effect?

To this rather extraordinary claim, the Secretary of State for Defence replied,

> I agree with him that it is remarkable that we have not received more casualties and greater losses than we have. It has been a remarkably successful venture.[31]

Note the use of the word 'remarkable'. When unexpectedly high losses are incurred because the enemy attacks with greater success than anticipated, one notes that given the success of the enemy attack, or given his potential, it is *remarkable* that the losses are so low. Precisely the same callousness can be found in one of Churchill's descriptions of a German night attack on London. He devotes most of it to the fires in Pall Mall and the destruction of the Carlton Club, and concludes,

> Altogether it was a lurid evening, and considering the damage to buildings it was remarkable that there were not more than five hundred people killed and about a couple of thousand injured.[32]

How remarkable.

There was insufficient protest from the press itself, which bowed all too slavishly to military direction. Here also there is a history. On the first day of the battle of the Somme, the great attack by Britain's volunteer army saw nearly 20,000 killed and nearly 60,000 wounded, on its own side. It was one of the most murderous and stupifying military debacles of all times. *The Times* reported, 'It is on balance a good day for England ...'.[33] The reporter who wrote this later justified himself by saying, 'I have to spare the feelings of men and women, who have sons and husbands still fighting in France'. Doubtless he meant well. But we should note that in 1916 General Haig had said that he would break off the offensive if it did not succeed immediately, yet the obsequiousness that surrounded him allowed him to continue the futile attacks for another four months, until British losses alone mounted to over 400,000.[34] How many mothers's feelings would have been spared if an early outcry had stopped the slaughter? Yet we can still read the same old apologetics today. In the *Guardian* of 3 July 1982, for example, Gareth Parry:

> The presentation of the Falklands war has been carefully sanitized. Pictures and descriptions of the casualties have been discreet, and I believe rightly, for the sake of relatives. Even now to attempt to describe some of the more horrific sights and sounds of war would be unkind.

Such is the way that we are prepared even now for the next war, with kindness.

6 A War in the Third World

IN THE beginning many spectators around the world were convinced that it was all *opera bouffe*: gauchos in ponchos and Brits in bowler hats snarling at one another and rattling a few sabres, before being led off to the conference table by their common American master. Instead, there *was* a short war which has rattled a good many preconceptions about contemporary world politics. It has certainly shaken the conventional wisdom that European 'imperialism' is a dead letter as well as the notion that the superpowers effectively 'control' all the military actions of their subordinates. Just as important, the Falklands conflict has also lifted a window on the political causes of war in the Third World through which we must briefly look.

There are two respects in which Galtieri's invasion bears remarkable parallels with other acts of aggression in the past few years. The Junta's seizure of the Falklands stemmed from growing public opposition to its tyranny at home. It was a blatant attempt—three days before a threatened general strike of Argentina's still powerful unions—to quiet opposition and secure a cheap popular triumph. Indeed the initial, easy successes were immediately presented as a nationalist legitimation of the military's control of government (although most of the population apparently saw this manoeuvre for what it was). Thus the first and most imperative reason for the Junta's impetuous action was its need to defuse internal tensions and boost its own collapsing support.

But there was a second, and more calculated, reason as well. The defeat of the token British garrison at Port Stanley was intended to symbolize Argentina's new prowess as a regional power. The decision to take the islands by force was meant to add credibility to Argentinian claims on the Antarctic as well as to intimidate its traditional rival, Chile. The Junta, victim of its own bombastic ideology, tried to counter domestic economic collapse with the escalation of Argentina's military pretensions. To this extent the invasion of the Falklands was a reflex of the same *hubris* which had led the Junta to despatch 'advisers' to Central America to fight there as proxy Yanquis. Internal control and military expansionism—the Junta's real *raison d'être* for invading the Falklands—had nothing to do with the sentiment of Argentina's population about sovereignty over the Malvinas. On the contrary, the invasion was an attempt to exploit the reasonableness of the country's claim so as to mobilize the issue for other, utterly ignoble aims.

The best riposte to the Junta came from the 'Mothers of the Plaza de Mayo'. Since 14 May 1978, every Thursday, their heads in white scarves, the mothers of those who have disappeared—presumed kidnapped and murdered by the regime—stand in Buenos Aires's 'Place of May'. They have done so every week since then, whatever the weather and the harassment; organized by the solidarity of common bereavement. They are the living indictment of the Junta and its associated killers, men like Menendez, the commander of the Argentine garrison in the Falklands, and the other thugs who came to power through making war against their own people. After the invasion, the mothers wrote on the placards placed around their necks as they stood in vigilance, 'The Malvinas belong to Argentina and so do the disappeared ones'.

This eloquent and moving symbol of resistance to the Junta is a reminder of the unpopular aspect to the capture of the Falklands. In a fully anti-colonial struggle such as the many we have witnessed since 1945, the armies which meet each other in combat are quite different in kind. A people's army and a colonial army may recruit from the same population. But one is already the arm of a state power, the other seeks to become the creator of a new state power. The essence of such a liberation struggle is the expression of this inequality. Its success depends upon the nationalist forces being able to make a sufficient strength out of their own conventional weakness and a sufficient liability of their opponent's conventional power, to overwhelm him in a political victory born of passage of arms. The conflict in the Falklands had none of *this* difference. It was a war between two conventional states, both of which attempted, through the battle of wills and weapons, to consolidate their unpopular regimes at home.

In so far as there is a familiar pattern to the colonial aspect of the Falklands confrontation, it dates back to the early nineteenth century. Then many wars took place between European states and already existing recognized states in what is now termed the 'Third World'—including an unsuccessful British siege of Buenos Aires in 1808. After the completion of colonial expansion, its consolidation and world wars, came the period of decolonization and the emergence of successful (because technologically and politically modern) resistance from within the imperial holdings, of France, Britain and Portugal especially. Today, the Argentinian attack on the Falklands, like the Indian takeover of Goa in 1961 or the Indonesian takeover of East Timor in 1976, is a sign that the boot it on the other foot. It is the turn of the once dominated to expand.

And despite their protestations of self-justification, there clearly is an element of colonialization to such moves.

Argentinian expansion is not imperialist, however; its ambition is limited to contiguous territory rather than any global reach. Recently, somewhat similar attempts by Third World states to expand their territorial dimension through war have occurred. In particular, since the end of the Vietnam War in 1975, there have been the Khmer Rouge attacks on Vietnam itself (from April 1977), the Somali attack on Ethiopia's Ogaden (July 1977), the Ugandan attack on Tanzania (November 1978) and the Iraqi invasion of Iran (September 1980). All four bear some parallels with each other and provide a comparative basis for defining the contemporary nature of the Argentine Junta's behaviour in seizing the Falklands. Of course, they are far from identical; it would be facile to seek some formula to which they could all be reduced. In each case the value of the contrast is that it helps to highlight the unique, indigenous and specific aspects of each conflict by allowing the common backdrop to be seen more clearly. But the background itself is also interesting.

If we tabulate each set of protagonists by smaller and larger country, the following common elements can be identified:

SMALLER		LARGER
Cambodia (Pol Pot)	vs	*Vietnam* (Le Duan's Politbureau)
Somalia (Siad Barre)	vs	*Ethiopia* (Mengistu, Haile Mariam)
Uganda (Idi Amin)	vs	*Tanzania* (Julius Nyerere)
Iraq (Saddam Hussein)	vs	*Iran* (Ayatollah Khomeini)

In each case the smaller country initiated hostilities against the larger one. In each, the smaller country was led by a harsh dictatorship which based its rule on terror, and continues to do so in the cases of Somalia and Iraq. The nature of the regime in the smaller state was also relatively and qualitatively *more* imposed and dictatorial than that in the society it attacked. It is not that Vietnam, Ethiopia, Tanzania or Iran today are democracies, they are not. But their respective regimes are the product of an authentic revolutionary mobilization, and the leaders of all the four larger states listed here have a national record and a base of support within the population that accords them 'legitimacy'. By contrast, those of the left hand side of the table, the smaller and more bellicose regimes, have been the product of rigid family dictatorships. Torture, massive terror, the disappearance of thousands, the cult of the personality and even the overt acknowledgement of such barbarism, rather than popular movements have marked these states.[1] There can be little doubt that the internal instability generated by such rule determined their attempts at military adventure. This is not to say that the four larger states are unfamiliar with violent state repression or are 'innocents' in the tensions that arose between the neighbouring pairs. In each case the dispute had a history on both sides and the smaller state had reason to fear the pressure and influence of the larger. The response however was reckless rather than cautious.

It is not difficult to see that the impetus of the Galtieri Junta, with tens of thousands of victims behind it, shared some of the characteristics of the other four aggressors. In each case, it should be added, a justifiable claim could be made out for the action taken. Probably the majority of the population in Cambodia, Somalia, Uganda and Iraq thought that the territory their army entered was theirs for reasons of history. This should warn us against any simple agreement with the passions of the Argentinians for the Malvinas. But whatever the rights and wrongs of the disputes, in all *five* cases a militaristic dictatorship took unilateral military action against a more powerful and somewhat more democratic, or at least a more rooted, regime.

The analogy seems to end at this point because, while Britain might be a more democratic state at present than Argentina, is is not a Third World country nor a recent site of revolutionary mobilization. Far from the war between Buenos Aires and London being a conflict between newly independent societies, it was against the ancient colonial regime—Britain—which historically dominated, even if it did not absolutely rule, its one time protégé Argentina. The war over the Falklands was a North/South clash, not a South/South one like the four just enumerated.

The Galtieri Junta, however, had not intended to tangle with the British militarily. It believed that no such response would be forthcoming. Argentina's military was certainly under the impression that the United States would either lean towards it in the conflict or remain strictly neutral, in either case this would have made it impossible for Britain to mount a credible military reaction.[2] One remarkable piece of evidence for the casual assumption of a peaceful takeover by the Junta is the amount of military equipment they had on order but still undelivered. Had they waited a year, they would have had twice as many French 'Super Etendards' with many more 'Exocet' missiles; a perhaps decisively larger number of German submarines would also have been at their disposal. Argentina's Air Force had not even acquired the extra fuel tanks for its 'Skyhawks' which would have given them time for more than a single pass over the islands. At the same time, Britain had disclosed plans to run down its surface navy. By 1984 London might not have been able to send an Armada. In addition the absence of serious preparations for a British landing, even after the Armada set out, shows that Argentina thought the idea of a war farcical rather than inevitable. Alas, it is one of the signs of truly irrational behaviour to presume the rational response of others.

But while the Junta had not considered the feelings of the British Parliament when it ordered the conquest of the Malvinas, it was aware of possible repercussions in Latin American capitals. Argentina was too weak to risk a war with Brazil. It had a pretext to fight Chile over some tiny islands, but Catholic opinion and US diplomacy had prevented it from doing so, while such a war might be drawn out and expensive. Yet the Junta desired to show the rest of Latin America that Argentina had recovered from the traumas of domestic strife since the death of Peron. The reappropriation of the Falklands seems to have been chosen as a symbolic substitute. Argentinian prowess would be demonstrated by pecking the tail of the mangey lion. It was not the lion itself they wished to brave. Rather they wanted to crow over the menagerie that struts in the other presidential palaces and barracks of their unhappy sub-continent. The Junta's aggression was of the South/South kind, in that its prime motivation was as a display aimed to impress its neighbours. It was displaced onto a bleak archipelago; one that happened to be the nominal possession of an erstwhile capital of Empire whose leadership was suffering from acute withdrawal pains.

What are the reasons for the wars of the Third World that have just been enumerated? They are by no means the only armed conflicts in the world's 'South' that have been or are taking place in our time. But they demonstrate a degree of independence from the postwar geopolitical order. At the same time they reproduce it in new ways. There are at least three reasons for such wars, the first of which—the arms trade—clearly imposes a new kind of dependency between 'North' and 'South', inherited from the old, more direct forms of hegemony.

(1) Much has been written about the export of high-technology military equipment from the armament centres of the great and once great powers. All the four wars listed above were fought with weapons manufactured in other countries, whether from the Western or Soviet blocs. In none of the conflicts was either one of the pairs of combatants capable of manufacturing the major weapon systems they deployed. These were indeed wars seeded and nurtured from outside. The terms by which the arms deals were transacted could differ. Sometimes the weaponry was acquired on credit, sometimes as outright aid, sometimes as in the Iraq-Iran war it was mostly acquired for cash—which gave the belligerents a significantly greater degree of political autonomy. But however they were obtained financially, the fact remains that without the external

supply the conflicts could not have taken place in the way they did. The shipment of weapons from North America, Europe, the Soviet bloc and China has proved to be the precondition for a rash of terrible small wars. Furthermore, there is a systemic logic to the transfer of armaments in this fashion, in addition to the political decisions which dominate the trade. Once one neighbour has modern weapons, then the other 'needs' to acquire them for self-defence. As each successful war leads to a victory and defeat, so the example of the fate of the vanquished and the new conquests of the victor motivate their surrounding neighbours to further purchases.[3]

(2) At the same time as many Third World countries have become dependent upon outside sources for their arms, they have also begun to demonstrate a degree of independence backed by their new military capacities. Argentina is only one example of this trend, whereby weapons bought from a number of suppliers have ensured an absolute dependency on none. But even when there is a single supplier of arms from outside, the recipient can strike further than the donor might desire. China probably did not want Pol Pot to persist in being quite so reckless. The Soviet Union assured Ethiopia that Somalia would not attack the Ogaden with its Russian supplied army. Autonomy can increase even when the means of destruction are only imported.

Perhaps the most remarkable sign of this was the war between Iraq and Iran. When most of the world's attention was concentrated upon the spectacular confrontation in the South Atlantic, the battle for Khorramshahr proceeded. Tens of thousands of troops battled each other along the fault lines of Arab and Persian, Sunni and Shi'ite within the Islamic World. The battle may still prove to be a decisive turning point. The Iranian victory, paving the way for a counter-invasion of Iraq, has shifted the balance of power within the Middle East and thus the world's chief oil exporting region; it will also have a profound effect on the geopolitical position of the Soviet Union, which borders Iran and is fighting inside Afghanistan to its east. What is perhaps most unusual about the Iraq-Iran war, given its importance, is that neither side has the support of the United States in any direct fashion. Indeed, both are clearly independent of the two great powers, rather than dependent upon either one of them, despite the fact that their armed forces were originally created thanks to Washington and Moscow.

(3) There is a third aspect to the conflicts between developing states. This is the way in which the burden of a top-heavy, 'modernized' state machine is socially unstable. Incapable of leading their socially divided, backward economies to a stable capitalist democracy; unwilling to open the way to a drastic socialization of the economy; unable to arouse the kind of popularity

a properly fascist state can mobilize; trapped by the tremendous economic, political and cultural pressures of the rest of the world, which bear down on an inevitably proud 'new' country with terrific force—many of these regimes turn to militarization and terror. The arms provide the means; political independence provides the opportunity. The unstable military dictatorship which may result provides the impetus, as it seeks to *preserve itself* by exploiting the combination of means and opportunity to strike outside its borders.

Wars initiated by a Third World state that attacks across its defined border are only one variant amongst a constant rash of conflicts which can be observed in almost all the world's regions. As the British threw their ring around Port Stanley, N'jamena fell to a rebel army in Chad, as Gaddafi withdrew, while Israeli forces bombed and shelled Beirut. A major Soviet offensive was taking place in Afghanistan. The Pol Pot forces had suffered severely from a Vietnamese campaign in their Thai-supplied bases inside Cambodia. The whole balance of force in the Middle East was threatened by the Iranian victory. Meanwhile the efforts of the Polisario in the Western Sahara and, possibly most important of all, the struggle in El Salvador, continued. We should not forget to mention the consolidation of Indonesian supremacy in East Timor, which it is forcibly incorporating into its territory after the most clear-cut case of genocide in recent times—a genocide materially supported by the same Anglo-Saxon countries which fought for the 'self-determination' of the Kelpers: Britain, the USA, Australia. At least 200,000 civilians out of less than one million were starved to death in East Timor.[4]

To bring such divergent terrors into a single global canvas would be beyond the unifying imagination of a contemporary Goya. But we can imagine that each of the local belligerencies may be fed into a Pentagon computor, its specificity coded in terms of American interests. It will not be difficult to guess the cumulative result: these things get out of the West's control. Somehow, therefore, the capacity of the United States to impose its will through the technological might and co-ordinated skill of its men needs to be reinstated after Vietnam. Politically, the Falklands crisis seems to reinforce a legalistic ideology that restrains America from imposing its own wishes through armed expeditions. But the actual example of the British Armada could be different. It has 'shown' the world what the West can do through its intimidating example. One of the consequences of the Falklands expedition could be that it has so raised the force level of the West's response to 'misdemeanors', that subsequently it will appear quite mild if America sends just a few planes to El Salvador ... Thatcher may thus have helped to solve the crucial problem of successive American administrations since 1975, by making it acceptable once again to intervene abroad directly. Almost certainly the enthusiasm for co-operation with the British that the Pentagon has displayed stems from this possibility. As far as Britain is concerned, then, the Falklands conflict represents a novel escalation which does bear a resemblance, however miniature, to the US war in Vietnam.

The war between Britain and Argentina over the Falklands was a peculiar combination of different types of conflict. So far as Argentina is concerned, it can be seen as an example of a Third World war, of the sort described. So far as the UK is concerned it is in part a colonial 'war of defence' and also a post-colonial war of intervention. For both countries it is a frontier dispute which has come about because of the virtually uninhabitable nature of the Falklands. More than large enough to house a community, but not fertile enough to be the basis for an autonomously viable community that could become independent in its own right (a factor that will be discussed in the next chapter), the Falklands-Malvinas remained an eccentric spot, subject to overlapping claims. If one looks at any atlas of frontier disputes one sees a world covered with the rash of contention. The only region which appears to have settled its borders is Europe, where there are more frontiers to the square mile than any equivalent zone. Yet more blood has probably been lost to resolve the placement of these boundaries than anywhere else. Millions have been killed to reach 'agreement' about its various sovereignties we now see delimited in our atlases and car-maps. Furthermore, in many cases it was Europeans who drew up the borders that are now subject to contention in other continents. While wars are endemic to human society to date, the modern pattern of aggressive international nation-states is European in origin. The new wars between developing countries may be seen as one of Europe's gifts to the world, as armour and infantry are launched in surprise attack. Europe was not the first to cultivate the art of war in ancient times, but it pioneered its industrial application. Now the underdeveloped world is 'catching up', as its members seek their own national 'definition'. By holding on to the Falklands, the British government found itself entangled by just such a development and was drawn into a war in the Third World.

7   A Just Settlement?

ON 14 MAY *The Times* warned against any compromise solution. The Peruvian peace initiative was, in its view, a close call, as its terms came near to betrayal. The Task Force was off the Falklands and it was necessary to press on; not least because 'The crisis has shaken the British people out of a sleep, and the people, once woken, will not lightly forgive those leaders who rang the alarm and then failed to fulfil their responsibility ...' It would be more accurate to say that the British public had been caught napping. Will future historians really look back to April 1982 and see a people waking from a long sleep? Will they judge *The Times* to have provided notable guidance? Or will they see it as a 'top' sleepwalker distressed by the daylight?

Whatever the answer, the British 'tradition' of judicious intelligence showed little vitality through the crisis, while the propagandists for war had a field day and not just in the House of Commons. The greatest advantage of the Right and the war party was their quickness of reflex, not least as they moved in on concepts such as 'sovereignty', the 'right to self-determination', the sanctity of the British 'way of life', and the imperative that 'aggression should not pay'.

The Times editorial which asserted that the British people were now woken and determined not to retreat, was designed to muster support for the feature article on its facing opinion page by Enoch Powerll. He was jubilant:

> All of a sudden, thoughts and emotions which for years have been scouted or ridiculed are alive and unashamed. In both universities [a revealing phrase], where, until recently, anyone who mentioned 'sovereignty' or 'the nation' or 'the British People' would have been lucky not to have been rabbled, students discuss with respect and approval arguments and propositions which presuppose those very things.

It is noteworthy that a man who thinks there are only two universities in Britain worthy of mention, should regard himself as a spokesman for 'the British people'. But not all of his account is false, however slanted and triumphalist. Words like 'sovereignty' did indeed go virtually uncontested, as they were usurped by Powell and his kindred spirits.

The Left's response tended instead to dwell on the *hypocrisy* of Tories who suddenly took it upon themselves to denounce the 'fascist Junta' in Buenos Aires. It needs little exercise of the imagination to hear those *same* Tory voices a few months previously expressing a very different sentiment, in response to complaints that they should not arm a regime like Argentina's, which had 'disappeared' so many of its citizens. ('I agree that it has been awful for lefties and people like that Jewish fellow Timerman, but you know, old chap, there are plenty of us Brits out there, and a pretty thriving Anglo-American community, and they don't complain, far from it.')

Indeed, it was a simple matter to prove beyond question the hypocrisy of the House of Commons as it waxed indignant about the right to self-determination of the Kelpers. Both Labour and Conservative governments had, in succession, approved the wholesale removal of an equivalent island population from their remote homeland of Diego Garcia, lock, stock and barrel, and quite against their wishes. In 1966 there was an Anglo-American military agreement to make this Indian Ocean coral atoll available as a US military outpost. The island is much smaller than the barren Faklands archipelago, but its tropical setting makes it far more advantageous for settlement and subsistence. Yet once it became an Anglo-Saxon staging post in the cold war there was deemed to be no room for its inhabitants. So they were forcibly deported to Mauritius over a thousand miles away, and dumped in poverty for more than a decade until the final adjudication—ironically coincident with the beginning of the Falklands crisis—awarded them a mere £4 million for their confiscated home.[1] The size of the indigenous communities involved in both cases is almost the same: 1,200 deportees from Diego Garcia; 1,300 native-born resident Falklanders. Could it be any more obvious, therefore, that the bi-partisan attachment in the Commons to the *principle* of self-determination for small island communities does not exist, or at the very least, is racially selective?

In allowing the eviction of the Diego Garcians (to make way for US Marines) Parliament undoubtedly committed an action worse, both in principle and practical impact, than the Argentinian seizure of the Falklands. It may not be a formal act of aggression to remove one's 'own' island people from their homes, but as a unilateral act of force against people it clearly overshadows the behaviour of Argentina in the Falklands, where the invaders killed nobody and apparently tried to ensure at first that life went on more or less as before.

If we simply desire to score points, the House of Commons would lose, were it not that it has better access to the press and television. But is not such argument a diversion anyway? In terms of ya-boo, custard-pie politics, we can show that the parliamentarians are hypocrites. What is new? Such noises are in fact the stuff of Parliament itself and the whole British 'debating' tradition, with its empty sounds. Party leaders seek to have it all ways, and do so: that is what their politics is about. Just to expose their double standards, and leave it at that, will impale us—if we have some genuine attachment to the concerns involved. Politicians with a light touch and slipper fingers can manipulate talk about 'rights' and 'principles'. Those who desire to mean what they say, on the other hand, can handle such terms only with care and difficulty. Hence the awkwardness when we are confronted by Thatcherite appeals to international standards. She may be a hypocrite but we cannot easily evade the issues without appearing shabby and underhand. If it was wrong to expel the Diego Garcians, for example, it must also be wrong to surrender the Kelpers unprotected to the Junta.

There are four key questions posed by the debate over the Falklands conflict: (1) the inhabitants' right to 'self-determination'; (2) the nature of territorial sovereignty; (3) the inhabitants' right to freedom and the preservation of their way of life; and (4) the argument that 'aggression should not pay'. In order to argue out these four often ideological issues as they relate to the war in the South Atlantic, it will be best to debate them within the framework of what a genuinely just and realistic settlement might have entailed.

As I have indicated earlier, there were important pre-existing elements for a peaceful and democratic resolution of the problem. These could have been drawn upon to make a practical and principled settlement which could have encompassed:

(1) The ceding of formal sovereignty over the Falklands to Argentina, provided adherence to the following:

(2) The withdrawal of all Argentinian and British troops and police—the demilitarization of the area.

(3) Local self-government through an elected Falklands council in liaison with a civilian representative of the central government in Buenos Aires.

(4) The guarantee of the indigenous inhabitants' present rights of law, language, religion, speech, assembly and travel.

(5) The appointment of an International Control Commission to supervise these conditions.

Such an agreement would have ensured peace; it could have met the rational demands of both sides. Sovereignty is transferred to Argentina, yet the democratic rights of the local people are preserved (the legitimate core of any British objection to the forcible takeover). It is dangerous to over-simplify arguments into slogans, but the approach that I will try to justify here could be summed up by saying that the Argentinian flag should fly over the Falkland

Islands, but that the Junta's police should not be allowed their jurisdiction.

1. Self-Determination

By common consent today, sovereignty is a matter to be decided by the people: people themselves should be the arbiter of their national identity, this is the fundamental democracy which belongs to them. However much this might be denied in practice (while being proclaimed by leaders everywhere), the principle is of immense importance. It marks a fundamental, if as yet unrealized, step forward in the struggle for human emancipation from repression.

The immediate problem which the idea poses at its most general level is as mundane as the principle itself is lofty. Sovereignty may be something that belongs to the people, yet its actual shape is carved out in soil. The limits of sovereignty are defined in each case territorially. While the principle of self-determination is something exercised by people, its practical effect is to mark boundaries; land becomes the sacred definition of the democratic right. This in itself need not make for difficulties, provided there is a clear match of territorial demarcation and people who desire separate sovereignties. One of the ways in which determining sovereignty by popular consent can become difficult and often intractable is when the two aspects do not coincide and different peoples claim sovereignty in the same land.

There are at least three different kinds of 'self determination' even with respect to national sovereignty. The first, with which the notion is most commonly associated, is the granting or winning of national independence, usually from a colonial power. Full statehood is then symbolized by entry into the United Nations. Extraordinary inequities of representation have resulted. Vast, multinational conglomerates such as India or Indonesia have become single nation-states, while dozens of tiny communities have also entered the world arena with the same formal status. Many of these have been islands. Yet the Falklands have not been able to achieve even this sovereignty. Had this been possible—if the Falklands could have emerged as a viable, English-speaking nation-state—then whatever Argentina's claims and feelings, the independence of the Falklands as a South American country would have been legitimate.

It was not possible. Other small islands luxuriate in statehood. Grenada, for example, is very much smaller than the Falklands (137 square miles as compared to 4,700). Yet Granada has a population of around 100,000. It has even seen a popular, peaceful transfer of power in 1979 from an overtly capitalist to an avowedly socialist administration, a clear sign of genuine capacity for self-government, whatever else one might think. In Grenada there are peasants, capable of ensuring their own survival, and the community as a whole is large enough to have some degree of economic independence.

The Falklands community consists of no more than a small village with a few outlying hamlets. Except that it is not even that: it is a company settlement, entirely dominated by the external network of ownership and economic directives that established it originally. It is said by those who have been there that the Faklands have been maligned by their reputation for bleakness. Doubtless one could say the same for the moon, which is also beautiful but inhospitable. Basically, the Falklands are at the edge of being uninhabitable; even trees can barely grow there so unrelenting are its winds. Only a company that sought to make a tidy profit from the vast extent of its grazing, and a maritime power that desired to control its harbour (mainly to prevent its use by enemy shipping), could ensure a degree of settlement. Among its inhabitants the administration, the local officials and pastor and the clerks are mainly supplied from outside. Because the Falklands are thus exploited on a global basis, some were needed locally to live there. But they could not establish themselves as a viable, autonomous community. Indeed, even as a sheep station, the Falklands are sinking into desuetude. Hence the implausibility of the present inhabitants forming a self-governing Falklands nation. There are only 1,300 native born residents on the islands at present, of which about 300 are children. 600 families can hardly form a country. Nor, sensibly, do they want *self*-determination. In 1980 the islanders sent an 'Earnest Request' to the Prime Minister asking her 'to reconsider the terms of the British Nationality Bill in order to accord full British citizenship to all the islanders of British descent'. (Their plea was rejected.)

The second type of demand for 'self-determination' is the important one claimed by 'stateless peoples' such as the Kurds, Basques, Biafrans or Palestinians. Their only relevance to this discussion is that when groups like the Kurds, for example, span territorial borders, their demand for their own sovereignty also becomes an external issue for the bordering states.

The third type of disputed 'self-determination' is that which comes about when the territorial claims of two states overlap and the allegiance of communities in one extend to the other (as in Ulster). The Falklands dispute is a variant of this type, as the British Government bases the defence of its control over the Falklands not on the grounds that the islands are part of the UK, whatever its inhabitants might think, but rather that its inhabitants desire to remain under the Crown whatever Argentina might propose. The question of principle here, then, is whether a local community subject to 'overlap' has the 'right' to determine *which* sovereignty it should come under; or whether, because that community is not itself demanding its own sovereignty, its fate can be ultimately decided by others.

Despite all the cant in the House of Commons, it is a choice irony that its own 'Churchillian' experience demonstrates that the wishes of the local community need not be regarded as sacrosanct. Take for example this argument in *The Times*: 'the wishes of the population concerned would seem to be a *decisively important* element in any solution that can hope to be regarded as permanent' (my emphasis). Is this not a well-rounded formulation of the right to self-determination of a community such as the Falklands? Yet the reader should pause for reflection if he or she nodded with agreement. For this quote from a *Times* editorial does not in fact concern the Falklands. In this instance it actually is writing about something as important as the outbreak of the Second World War. The passage comes from the conclusion to its lead editorial of 7 September 1938, which argued the merits of appeasement. It reads in full:

> In any case the wishes of the population concerned would seem to be a decisively important element in any solution that can hope to be regarded as permanent, and the advantages to Czechsolovakia of becoming a homogeneous state might conceivably outweigh the obvious disadvantages of losing the Sudeten German districts of the borderland.

The argument was the central 'principled' expression of appeasement of which *The Times* was an advocate; it was the intellectual justification for the Munich agreement which soon followed. What happened was simple enough in broad outline. Over two million ethnic Germans lived inside the borders of Czechoslovakia, in the Sudetenland. They were predominantly sympathetic to the German state and demanded their full national 'rights' as Germans. The Czechs naturally opposed such demands and attempted to limit the autonomy of the local population. Hitler sought to support them. 'Appeasement' was the agreement by the British and French governments to allow the Sudeten Germans the 'right' to self-determination and hence to affiliate to the *Reich*.[2] This dismembered Czechoslovakia by depriving it of its critical, defensible mountain border and much of its armaments industry, and left it exposed to subsequent German action (it made it a 'homogenous state', with 'obvious disadvantages ...').

It is clear today that whatever local, community self-government the Sudeten Germans should have been allowed, they should not have been granted 'self-determination' when this meant their affiliating to the sovereignty of their 'kith and kin'. Historically, then, it is amusing that those who argue against the Falklanders' wishes being paramount in determining their national identity, should be the ones charged with 'appeasement'. For in fact those who favoured appeasement, and decisively weakened Britain's position in 1938 by allowing the dismemberment of Czechoslavkia, were precisely those who argued that the wishes of a local community *should* determine its national allegiance. By 16 September 1938, Chamberlain was convinced that self-determination was the 'only solution'. He defended his concessions on the grounds that 'Hitler did not want more than self-determination',[3] and the Munich agreement itself was signed two weeks later. Yet in their urge to re-emphasize the 'lessons' of that time, those who support the British war in the South Atlantic have gone even further than warning us against another 'appeasement'. In *Authors Take Sides on the Falklands*, two contributors specifically mention the Sudetenland, in the belief that it supports their case. Bevis Hillier says of the Argentine takeover, 'There *is* principle at stake—the same principle as was at stake when Hitler invaded the Sudetenland and Czechoslovakia.' While in even more trenchant terms, David Holbrook equally makes nonsense of history as he argues that, 'the government's action was right, and the only possible one'. 'As for the British Left!', he continues, 'They have responded despicably! Have they forgotten the Spanish War and non-intervention? Have they forgotten the Sudetenland and appeasement?'[4]

It should not be suggested that Neville Chamberlain was any more deeply attached to the real principle of self-determination than Margaret Thatcher. On the contrary, the Cabinet minutes of the time apparently reveal his political selectivity in this respect. 'Speaking personally, the Prime Minister said that he did not object to the principle of self-determination, or, indeed, attach very much importance to it. What he wanted was a fair and peaceful settlement. It was the practical and not the theoretical difficulties of the situation which concerned him.'[5] We can be sure that Thatcher felt exactly the same way over Zimbabwe.

Indeed, we can say that the Second World War established as a cardinal principle that communities do *not* have the exclusive right to determine which state they should be affiliated to, and that their wishes have to be balanced against geo-political realities and other human rights. In general, rights anyway cease to be meaningful when abstracted from circumstances; principles are needed as guides to the complexities of the world not as a means of liquidating them. In addition, even on its own terms the demand of the Falklanders is ambiguous. They may call for continued rule from London, but that also means that London is entitled to exercise its sovereignty according to its own definition of its interests, and may thus dispose of the islands should it so wish. The UK's sovereignty cannot be unilaterally arbitrated by the Falklands population alone. While attention must be paid to the needs of the local people, neither philosophically, nor logically, nor historically, are we obliged to conclude that the Kelpers have the right to self-determination—especially if that means that the Falkland Islands must stay British.

2. Territorial Sovereignty

We can now see how the issue of self-determination has been confused in the Falklands crisis. The 'principle' is never absolute and it applies primarily to the rights of a definable community to its own nation-statehood. The case of the Falklands is one in which the local inhabitants are not able to exercise their own self-determination, and as a consequence, by claiming an allegiance to a far-away state, have created a question of overlapping sovereignties on the ground. This means that because the Falkland Islands is not a country or a potential country on its own, it has to belong to some *other* country in terms of sovereignty. Its sovereignty, then, is relative. It belongs either to Britain or to Argentina. I will argue that in this case it should be regarded as the possession of the latter. But this is strictly an argument by default. The Falklands are Argentinian *rather than* British, because they cannot credibly be independent. It is a relative argument of geography and sentiment, not of history and morality.

In terms of geography, the Falklands do not belong to Argentina merely because the islands are part of the Argentinian continental shelf. By that argument, Britain would have the right to overrun Ireland, and France the right to take its revenge on Britain for the defeat of Napoleon. The geographical argument is overwhelming in its actuality, only because if the islands have to belong to one country or another as a dependency, then clearly they should belong to that country of whose continental shelf they form a part, *rather than* a country more than 6,000 miles away in the other hemisphere.

So far as opinion is concerned, Argentina bases its claim to the islands upon history. The Malvinas were taken from them by the British 150 years ago, and as Latin Americans they recognize the Hispanic borders of their continent only. To accord any legitimacy to such an argument is both dangerous and absurd. The world would be at war for another 150 years if every such contention were re-opened. Mexico's claim on Texas is far stronger than Argentina's claim on the Falkland Islands. Similarly, China would have a case to make out for Siberia; Poland on the Ukraine; Germany on Poland. Nationalist sentiments rooted in a partly mythological, partly accurate version of the past, should not sway us. One people's version of history, however passionately felt, will disparage and belittle the history experienced by other peoples. Argentina's nationalist perspective is no reason in itself for conceding sovereignty.

There is, however, good reason to take those feelings into account in one practical sense: *They* exist today. What other attitudes should be balanced against them? Whatever the Mexicans might feel about Texas, Americans know that Texas belongs to the USA. In the case of the Falklands, however, there is no such balance of sentiment. Had you asked any number of Argentinians at the beginning of this year about the Falklands, they would have told you the Malvinas belonged to them. That is not to say that they would have endorsed a reckless takeover designed to divert popular attention from Argentina's economic plight. But whatever their political belief, its people regard the Falklands as part of their land. Had you asked any British citizen by contrast, most would not even have known where you were talking about.

In her Cheltenham speech, Thatcher asked, 'Why do we have to be invaded before we throw aside our selfish aims ...'. But were 'we' ever invaded in Britain? Even after the Falklands War this assertion seems bizarre; before it would have been incomprehensible. On the afternoon that Argentina seized the islands, for example, would an MP have telephoned his mistress to say, 'I'm afraid tonight's off darling, we've been invaded'? If he had, he would certainly have been open to misinterpretation. Yet soon after the event, in *New Society* Adam Roberts considered the question from the point of international law and wrote with academic solemnity: 'The Argentine invasion of the Falkland Islands imposed a foreign military occupation regime on a part of British territory for the first time since the Second World War.'[6] The same point was repeated fanatically by Enoch Powell. But it has a strange, deeply imperial ring. For the Falklands are only British territory in the sense that they are a British possession. They are not part of Britain. Thus there is a massive inequality of popular sentiment in Argentina and Britain respectively, over the fate of the Falklands. This is and will remain a decisive factor in the resolution of their ultimate destiny.

The case for saying that the Falklands are Argentina's is firm. There was an act of aggression by the Junta, but it was not territorial aggression. Sooner or later, we can be sure that eventually Argentina's flag will be raised over them with general international recognition, whether or not other flags, such as that of the UN or even the Union Jack fly beside it. Nonetheless, the assignation of sovereignty is not a straightforward matter. The case is complicated in a central and important respect by the wishes and feelings of the existing islanders.

3. Restoring 'Freedom' to the Falklands

'*Even though* the position and circumstances of the people who live in the Falkland Islands are uppermost in our minds ...' Michael Foot said nothing of their actual circumstances. One scours the great debate of 3 April for relevant detail. Rowlands said that the people there discussed even obscure Parliamentary questions, which would make the Kelpers one of the most idiosyncratic and articulate communities on earth. Other evidence contradicts this unlikely idea. So before considering what it means to say that the British are 'liberating' the Falklanders (Thatcher), or seeking to ensure their 'freedom' (Hattersley), perhaps we should enquire into the realities of their 'marvellous' British way of life.

A major source is the Shackleton Report of 1976, undertaken by a survey team headed by Lord Shackleton, son of the famous polar explorer.[7] Its purpose was to make an inventory the resources of the islands and ascertain their potential for development. Because it argues the case for investment in the Falklands in a professional manner, the Report strives to be objective about the problems while also seeking to put prospects in the best possible light. Thus it is frank about the bleak future for sheep-raising on the islands, even though this currently generates 99% of the colony's exports (p. 31). Due to poor soil, hostile weather and a decline in the quality of the grassland, the local wool industry 'has been in slow but steady decline since 1919' (pp. 118-23). On the other hand, not to miss the positive side of the picture, the Report notes that 'Penguins also help to improve the vegetation by their trampling activity' (p. 87).

The main theme of the Shackleton Report is dependency: the dependency on the Falkland Islands Company for trade, and the personal and psychological dependency of the people who live there, many virtually enserfed to its domain. Economically, the colony is 'a territory totally dependent on imports for most of its consumption and capital goods' (p. 31). The Falkland Islands Company (FIC) exercises a virtual monopoly over land (of which it owns 40%), shipping, auctions (which decide the price of wool) and banking (p. 19). In Port Stanley, 'there is little choice of employers' (p. 79) and the FIC-owned 'West Store' dominates retailing with two-thirds of all sales in Stanley and half of the sales in the islands (p. 243). Between 1955 and 1975 the Company transferred £5 million to the United Kingdom in profits (p. iv). That might not sound like very much, but at the rate of £250,000 a year, it meant in 1974 the equivalent of more than 20% of the total income of all the inhabitants. This, however, seems to be more a measure of the poverty of the majority of the Falklanders than an index of the lucrative situation of the Company.

What, then, is life like for the people who live there? The

Falklands community seems to have been, before the recent war, a highly stratified and divided set of groups, as small communities often tend to be. In this instance the dependence on a single export product, itself controlled in the main through large holdings run by managers with a workforce of farmhands, must have exacerbated matters. The presence of government administrators posted from Britain, with much higher educational levels than the low standards found amongst the indigenous people, also added to this internal sense of strong social divisions (p. 81). The Shackleton Report gives the following table, based on Falkland Islands Government information, of the 914 registered incomes, in 1974.

Income Range (£)	Total No.
below 500	130
500–999	253
1.000–1,499	303
1,500–1,999	106
2,000–2,499	59
2,500–2,999	22
3,000–3,499	15
3,500–3,999	5
4,000–4,499	8
4,500–4,999	1
Over 5,000	12
Total Number	914
Total Income	£1,173,905
Average Income	£1,284

The exact population of the Falklands was not known in 1982, but the 1980 census showed 1,813 residents of whom 302 were born in Britain. The 914 incomes listed seem to include some of those of the temporary or posted residents working in the Falklands for some years. It can be assumed that these would lie in the higher income brackets; almost certainly, the 600 incomes below £2,000 a year went to Kelper families. The Report states (p. 81):

Most native born islanders of what they themselves call 'the working class' live in conditions of dependence, which are attractive in immediate and material terms but which offer no encouragement for engagement in economic, social or political development, since scarcely any of them have a stake in the place. This applies as much at the collective as at the individual level. Apart from the right to vote for the small group of people who make up the Legislative Council (dominated, at least numerically, by farm owners and managers) they have no real opportunity to influence decisions on public affairs.... It is clear that the distinctly low educational standards in the Islands leave locally taught people at a disadvantage in dealing with farm managers/owners and UK recruited persons, heightening the sense of dependence and relative inferiority.

This general condition worried the Shackleton team, which realized that community values had to be 'stimulated', especially among locally born people, for there to be any sustained economic development of the Falklands. These people had important qualities:

> They include honesty, versatility, physical hardiness and a capacity for sustained effort. Yet there appear to be other less encouraging features, such as a lack of confidence and enterprise at the individual and community level, and a degree of acceptance of their situation which verges on apathy. (p. 74)

Various social factors reinforce this unsatisfactory situation. Because of the remoteness of the communities and the difficult terrain, there is little interaction between isolated settlements or even between the different groups within Port Stanley. In some country areas, 'the quality of life is distinctly low' (p. 79). This is made worse by the fact that, 'the sex structure of the population is remarkable for its lack of females' (p. 15). One consequence is a high rate of marital instability. In the outlying settlements,

> It is common for 'the big house' to have the only voice contact with the outside world (usually by radio telephone). In these cases the farm workers must approach the manager or owner in any situation however personal, requiring early action from beyond the settlement, e.g. in regard to medical advice.

The result is that,

> Although the attitude of most managers/owners is certainly benevolent, it may also be described as paternalistic. (Indeed, more than one manager told us that it might sometimes appear feudal.) (p. 76)

It is therefore not surprising that young people especially have been leaving the Falklands, 'in search of a greater degree of personal freedom' (p. 77). What future could they look forward to?

> Indeed, the situation as regards community spirit and cohesion was perhaps well put to us by one resident when he said simply, 'There is no glue' (p. 80).

It will be remembered that in the debate on the Falklands of April 3, Thatcher said, 'The people of the Falkland Islands, like the people of the United Kingdom, are an island race. Their way of life is

British....' And Michael Foot thundered back: 'The people of the Falkland Islands have the absolute right to look to us at this moment of their desperate plight.' After glancing at the official report of their situation, one wonders whether this should not have been said with equal fervour *before*, rather than after, Argentina's invasion.

Members of Parliament, however, seek to protect Britain's standing in the world, clearly a more pressing duty than spending one new pence worth of concern on conditions in the colonies. So it is not surprising that a part-owner of a Falkland farm stated: 'Most of the people on the islands believe that under the Argentine flag the islands can be developed and improved.'[8] Indeed, under the headline 'Sheep shearer changes sides', we were told about one Kelper who took out Argentinian nationality. According to his girl friend, 'He wanted Argentina to have the islands because life there is so boring.'[9] Argentina did indeed provide more excitement, for it seems he was jailed soon after its defeat.

If Britain was fighting for the 'freedom' of the islanders, what was the power structure of the Falklands? The colony was ruled by a Governor appointed by Britain. He was advised by a 'Legislative Council' of eight, six of whom were elected by the islanders (the other two were *ex officio*). But the real ruling 'body' seems to have been an Executive Council in which not even the Legislative Council had a majority. Of the six on the Executive body, two were the Governor's appointments, two *ex officio* and the other two came from the Legislative Council. The Falklands did not have democratic government by any stretch of the imagination at the ruling level. There has been some attempt at 'popular' improvement. Being a British community it has a trade union and once saw a strike for higher agricultural wages. (Could this mean that the Kelpers are stubbornly set in their old-fashioned practices—like the train drivers?) At any rate, political representation made little headway. The Stanley Town Council, which Shackleton describes as 'one of the very few potential counter-weights to government' (p. 74) was, alas, 'abolished a few years ago' (p. 81). We are not told by whom, but perhaps its demise was connected with the fact that a 'National Progressive Party' on the islands proved to have 'only a brief life'. It seems probable that efforts to initiate a genuine autonomous polity foundered on the company's stranglehold and the Falklands' economic decline, accompanied by the demographic drain of its youth. Today, much of the actual Kelper population of Stanley consists of retired people who, after a lifetime of labour in the 'camp' (the local term for the countryside, from the Spanish *campo*), invest their savings in a clapboard house.

As for the Falkland Islands Company itself, it was taken over by a subsidiary of the asset-stripping specialists Slater Walker, in 1972, and duly stripped of its assets. It was then sold to Charringtons, which was acquired by Coalite in 1977; its turnover currently represents 2% of Coalite's business. According to one discussion of the Falklands crisis, 'no islanders are now represented as either shareholders or directors of the company that now controls the FIC. Indeed, on 26 February 1982, just over a month before the war, the FIC decided at an extraordinary meeting that it would cease to be a publicly listed company, and thus is no longer obliged to publish even its basic information about the Islands' economy.'[10]

Of course, the Kelpers do have their 'Britishness'. Shackleton notes, 'the most striking example of solidarity has been the common feeling on the sovereignty issue.' In a society of remarkable apathy, one which 'has no glue', where managers describe their relations with their labourers as 'feudal', and which is kept together by the Company's interests—the *only* thing it seems to have is extra-hemispheric loyalty. 'They have been loyal to us. We must be loyal to them',[11] Thatcher insisted. Yet their national life is as empty of content as the Royal Wedding mugs placed loyally upon their dressers. Thatcher, who has destroyed community upon community in Britain itself has decided that the Kelper's way of life must be preserved at all costs. The Tory talk of saving the Falklands and 'restoring' its freedom is little more than a cruel manipulation of the pathetic dreams of a community long despised by London.

When their 'liberation' was complete, the stalwart messages of thanks and the kisses for the soldiers seen on television appeared to come from the farm managers and outside (British) nurses. When the surrender was announced, what 'should have been a moment for jubilation' was met merely with 'enigmatic reserve' by the Kelpers themselves.

> At times it was hard to believe that they (the Falklanders) had any connection with the war. They behaved, it sometimes appeared, like peasants caught in an eighteenth century European dynastic clash—getting on with their farming as best they could while the rival armies swarmed around them.[12]

Could this have been because, indeed, they did *not* have any real connection to the causes of the war, and that the conflict was nothing more than a clash of sovereignty? Perish the thought! Yet another reporter observed the same phenomenon:

> The islanders never seemed particularly glad to see us, although that could be put down to their natural reserve and shyness with strangers ... More often than not they went about their daily lives as if the troops swarming around them did not exist.[13]

At last, however, 'there seems little doubt that change is imminent', *The Times* reporter noted; a garrison is being considered which will 'treble the population of the Falklands and put civilians in a minority'. And so the islanders are coming to realize, 'that they are still an occupied people, albeit this time occupied by their own forces'. Not unnaturally, 'bitter words (are) being exchanged between locals and soldiers'.[14]

Perhaps not so many words. The sceptical passivity of the islanders and their apparent lack of enthusiasm in their new situation may be measured perhaps by the first town meeting to take place in Stanley after its 'liberation'. It did not receive much attention in the British press. But *Time* magazine reported that the organizer said he was 'disappointed' at the attendance, while in addition, 'Although it lasted for two hours, most of the 100 townspeople who turned out were silent...'.[15] Simon Winchester found a similar attitude; hatred of Argentina after the invasion is now compounded by bitterness towards the British,

> Their attitude towards the British is a mixture of continued deep mistrust, disappointment and a sullen acceptance of the military realities of the new occupying army amongst them. Six weeks since liberation, and the Falklands people—as distinct from the Falklands establishment—are profoundly unhappy.

Few other journalists got beyond the press handouts to even see the distinction, let alone report it.[16]

I noted earlier the reports that the islanders were mostly left alone by Argentina's garrison. Why then should the British forces seem like occupying troops? Buried away, there were disturbing reports. The BBC's correspondent, Robin Fox, delivered some of the most fulsome panegyrics to the heroism of the '2 Para'. For example at Goose Green,

> The achievement of H. Jones and his men was heroism in battle on the scale of Leonidas and the men of Sparta at Themophylae.... As we crouched by the line of gorse bushes, the only landmark at that point, the unit seemed entirely cut off.[17]

Yet even he felt obliged to add at the bottom of another of his articles in the *Listener*, something that was given little emphasis in the mass media.

> I cannot pretend these men are angels. In Port Stanley, when the tension of battle was over the amount of 'proffing' by British troops was considerable—some understandable, some not, such as the thieving of a collection of gold coins from a young vet who had just lost his wife in the final bombardment.[18]

Perhaps because they were in the eye of the storm, many of the 'slow' and ill-educated Kelpers grasped what was happening long before the majority of the British public. Anthony Arblaster has described how the Kelper Jim Burgess was hustled away from the television camera by British officials when he stated that the islanders 'think they are being used, and I'm inclined to agree'. That was before the task force had arrived in the South Atlantic. Arblaster goes on to condemn the British action and in particular to denounce the way the 'rights of the islanders' were used by Thatcher's Government as 'an ideological and moral camouflage'. It is difficult not to agree.[19]

All the same, part of that camouflage was instinctive rather than deliberate falsification. Thatcher and Foot may genuinely believe that if the Falklanders want to be ruled by them, then that *is* a 'liberation'. For the inhabitants of the UK this perhaps is the more serious problem. As Thatcher told the broadcaster Jimmy Young:

> I am only here in the capacity for which I am here this morning because our people have the right to self-determination. Just let's get it right. This is what democracy is all about.

Got it? '*Our* people have the right to self-determination.' The word 'our' is ambiguous: in one sense it reaches out to include all Britons ('We have self-determination'), but it also pulls sharply inwards to the *possessive*, as in a remark between two Lords ('Our people are pretty slow off the mark, thank goodness'). To put it more empirically, it was widely noted that Cecil Parkinson MP, previously a figure of no public significance, was suddenly helicoptered into the War Cabinet and became its public spokesman, although he held no high office of state, and had only just been appointed by Thatcher as Chairman of the Conservative Party. But the composition of the British War cabinet itself received less scrutiny. If we leave aside the only occasional presence of the Attorney General, it seems that its participants were:

Elected Persons	*Non-Elected Persons*
Thatcher (Prime Minister)	Armstrong (PM's Office)
Pym (Foreign Affairs)	Wade-Gray (Civil Service)
Nott (Defence)	Palliser (Civil Service)
Whitelaw (Home Affairs)	Havers (Head, Diplomatic Service)
Parkinson (Conservative Party)	Lewin (Chief, Defence staff)

Clearly, some forms of self-determination are more determined than others.[20] Even the informed public in the UK can have only the haziest knowledge of half 'their' officials who presided over the war, if they have ever heard of them at all.

When the Tories and their supporting newspapers assert that the people of the Falklands Islands have been 'liberated', they mean to stand before the British electorate and say, '*we* are the liberators of

Britons. Therefore, we are *your* liberators.' The Falklanders themselves were merely the necessary cipher—all the more effective as a signifier for being as close to meaninglessness themselves as possible. The new language was nicely captured by a *Sunday Telegraph* post-Falklands editorial. It called for the 'emancipation' of workers from 'trade-union exploitation'.[21]

4. 'Aggression Should Not Pay'

This was the statement that carried most conviction. It was said with a righteousness of purpose, yet strangely, or perhaps not so strangely, it was also said with remarkable aggression. Various formulas were added before the landing and final assault on Port Stanley, such as 'we would prefer the Argentines to go peacefully but ...'. For many these were little more than a civilized decoration to a sentiment of gut, animal instinct. The latter was put with military succinctness by Sir Arthur Harris, Marshall of the RAF. Now aged 90 he was Chief of Bomber Command during World War Two. When the Vulcan bombers tried to hit the airstrip at Port Stanley, he appeared in full uniform bedecked with all his medals to tell reporters, 'We can't be kicked around without retaliating'.[22] After victory, Cecil Parkinson explained, 'To do our duty to our own people, and our duty to the whole civilized world, we have dispatched a Task Force of prodigious power'.[23] And one can feel in this formula the way the British Government has made a virtue out of retaliation. It came as a relief that at last the UK could be aggressive.

The issue produced one of the most fascinating tensions of the war. Its backers in the UK were bursting with delight at their conquests and were keen to pursue them with vigour during the conflict itself, yet had to appear in public as sober as a judge. This discrepancy allows for a more general reflection: history takes place in the demotic. In so far as decision makers are really the masters of events, they act and react in a vulgar and personal fashion. In so far as they make up their minds in discussion with close associates, these exchanges are livid with the crapulous feelings of those whose lives are dominated by the struggle for power. Yet even in confidential documents, let alone public speeches, their motives are presented in the finest prose they can achieve. Reasons of disinterest rather than self-interest are always foremost—in the public domain. On occasions in Parliament, a flicker of the actual drive behind the righteousness may be sensed. That is what made the 3 April debate so informative. One of the most forthright MPs did not speak then, however. Alan Clark is amongst the most hawkish of the war party on the Tory benches and undoubtedly activated the feverish violence amongst Conservatives after Argentina's takeover. As the British

Army was poised around Port Stanley, he told an interviewer that in his view the Falkland's war,

> has enormously increased our world standing. You asked about world opinion—I mean, bugger world opinion—but our standing in the world has been totally altered by this. It has made every other member of NATO say 'My God, the British are tough'.[24]

That is how Thatcher wants it too. Her objective internationally, but also at home and not least in Parliament, is to be thoroughly intimidating. She told an American TV audience, 'I have the reputation as the Iron Lady. I am of great resolve. That resolve is matched by the British people.'[25] And those Britons who do not 'match it' had better watch out.

On the international scene, this lesson hardly needs to be pondered. It was obvious that the British were able to push Argentina around because they had superior force. The response of one Brazilian opposition politican was to demand a crash programme for the construction of Brazilian nuclear weapons. Similarly *South* magazine, after noting that the Falklands War was a 'godsend' for Israel', asked why the 1,800 Falklanders should merit such a 'rescue' operation while 750,000 West Bank Palestinians do not, and concluded 'it is all a question of power in the end'. In *private*, those who sent the task force will agree, adding that what is also needed is that extra charismatic quality: will. The nerve to use force matters as much: one needs not only 'clout' but also 'toughness'. The prodigious power of the task force from the civilized world, to use Parkinson's description, was not engaged upon a civilizing mission. It taught Argentina a lesson; its pedagogy for Buenos Aires and for the rest of the world is 'might is right' and 'have a spirit of iron'.

Nonetheless, one could still argue that if Britain had not used force and had agreed to concede sovereignty over the Falklands to Argentina after 2 April, while seeking only to safeguard the life of the inhabitants and offer them compensation, then this also would have made it seem that 'might is right'. Argentina had gained something by force—wouldn't this show that aggression pays? There are two kinds of answers to such a question. The first is in terms of the dispute itself. The kind of resolution to the conflict which has been suggested and which may well be implemented in the future is one that provides for local government under nominal Argentine sovereignty. The idea is obvious enough, as *Newsweek* put it,

> The trick is to recognize Argentine sovereignty over the islands while preserving the islanders' right to govern themselves. The possible compromise: make the Falklands an autonomous region of

Argentina.... Argentina would have to give up posting its troops, teachers and policemen on the islands and guarantee the islanders' right to self-government.... Under such a scheme, the Argentines could claim to have vindicated their ancient claim to the islands. The British could be satisfied that London had honoured its promise to protect the islanders from dictators.[26]

Such an arrangement would not have 'rewarded' the Junta if international supervision had been imposed. What kind of advertisement would it have been to their own people, if the UN were deployed to ensure that part of the local population retains its rights to free speech and assembly? If the Malvinas can have 'democracy', the Argentinian people might have argued, why can't we? By insisting upon the withdrawal of the Junta's troops (which was conceded in the negotiations), and granting sovereignty to the country of Argentina. Britain (and the UN) could have demonstrated how negotiation and consent are preferable to the use of force.

But the second and larger answer to this question must be to challenge the pretentions that underlie the way it is posed. Iraq launched an unprovoked attack on Iran in 1980, and by the beginning of 1982 it was obvious to the whole world that—in a massive way—it had been shown that 'aggression did not pay'. Yet this did not deflect the Argentinian Junta. Indeed, it shows just how obtuse the world is in this respect that when Thatcher went to the United Nations to speak at its special disarmament session, it was generally felt that she was a female Begin. US interviewers questioned her along these lines but she rebutted the comparison. *He* was gulty of aggression (though it seemed to be 'paying'), while Britain had been acting in 'self-defence'.

The questioners were right. What lies behind Thatcher's strictures against aggression is an imperial notation that *favours* it. Parkinson argued,

Each success for the dictators sucks life from the democracies. Allow Argentina to make a colony of the Falklands and you make a potential prey of every little nation on earth.

Thus the democracies, of whom there are so few, must protect all the little nations, of whom there are so many. This is really an argument for the West's global dominion, albeit quietly put. A similar, subtle argument was put by the historian Trevor-Roper. He drew a comparison with 1770 when the Spanish Governor of Buenos Aires occupied the Falklands. According to Trevor-Roper, this action, which had the surreptitious encouragement of the French, threatened to upset the Treaty of Paris (1763), a Treaty which he regards as having 'settled the world' and as establishing the *Pax Britannica*. The British assembled a great fleet. The Spanish then relinquished the Falklands without a fight, but they did not renounce their claim to the sovereignty of the islands, which is why, apparently, they remain contested to this day. Trevor-Roper also argues that the British Government in 1770 (and Dr Johnson on its behalf) were right to resist demands that there had to be a war with Spain merely because it refused to endorse British claims on the Falklands. What was involved was the general 'principle' of the matter and the same is true today:

> The essential issue is the same.... That issue is not the possession of the islands ... nor the wishes of the islanders ...; it is the maintenance of real peace in the world.... If Spain had kepts its spoil in 1770 the signal would have been clear; the settlement of 1763 would have been everywhere at risk. Similarly, if Argentina had kept its spoil today, the rule of law would have been replaced by that of force and no undefended island would have been secure.[27]

Trevor-Roper lends all his distinction to what is evidently an imperialist world-view: behind the 'principle' that aggression shall not pay is a definition of peace—*Pax Britannica*—which was once the incarnation of global expansionism.

Hence also the foolishness of Michael Foot when he launched this argument in the first place in the House of Commons; that British 'deeds' were needed in the South Atlantic, 'to ensure that a foul and brutal aggression does not succeed in our world. For if it does, there will be a danger not *merely* [a choice formulation] to the Falkland Islands, but to people all over this dangerous planet.' In the same speech Foot also dismissed the idea that there is a 'colonial dependence or anything of the sort' involved in the Falklands. Yet any expedition by the UK to 'put matters straight' 7,000 miles away, necessarily reproduces *some sort* of colonial-style posture. Edward Thompson drew upon the real skills of a historian to see this truth about his own time and wrote soon after it began:

> The Falkland's war is not about the islanders. It is about 'face'. It is about domestic politics. It is about what happens when you twist a lion's tail ... [it is] a moment of imperial atavism, drenched with the nostalgias of those now in their later middle-age....[28]

Even nostalgia, it transpires, is capable of renovation. What has surprised many is the vigour and 'professionalism' with which the Thatcherites have pursued their transports into the past. Britain covered its tracks towards the military demarche with a plethora of diplomatic notes and concessions as the Government humoured those who desired a peaceful settlement. Manoeuvres by General Haig and at the UN seem to have been followed with alarm rather than desire by the War Cabinet. For example, after the landing at San Carlos, 'their fear of a ceasefire imposed by the UN appears to have led cabinet ministers to demand a premature push out from the beachhead ...'.[29]

Above all, the attack on the *General Belgrano* remains to be explained. It was sunk on 2 May by the British nuclear powered 'hunter-killer' submarine, the *Conqueror*. After the *Conqueror* sailed back into the Clyde on 3 July, flying the skull and crossbones traditional for a submarine that has just made a 'kill', its commander confirmed that the *General Belgrano* had been attacked thirty miles outside the British-declared 'total exclusion zone', apparently without a warning and under direct orders from Fleet headquarters in the UK. Not only had he been in constant touch with the Fleet Commander in Britain, but the final order to attack was confirmed by London. Over three hundred of Argentina's sailors died as the second ship in its fleet went down in 40 minutes, under the impact of two conventional torpedoes. Questioned by Healey, Nott admitted in Parliament that the *Belgrano* had been some hundreds of miles away from the British task force. It thus posed no immediate threat. Why, then, was it sunk? An interview given by the President of Peru sheds an interesting light, as he was very active in the peace negotiations and had come up with an intiative that the British had apparently been obliged to accept and which he felt Argentina was on the verge of agreeing to. The President thought that 'on 2 May we were very close to a settlement, which was frustrated with the sinking of the *Belgrano*.' And he continued:

> What was unfortunate was that violence impeded the accord. The very unfortunate sinking of the *Belgrano* at that very point also sank all the peace proposals we had made. This didn't have any justification. This was an act committed outside the area proscribed by Great Britain. And this created a very disagreeable climate. I still cannot console myself that the proposal I made wasn't approved the morning of May 2. With it we would have avoided the loss of the *Belgrano*, the loss of almost 400 young lives (on the ship) and the loss of the *Sheffield* and all the destruction that has come afterwards.[30]

Until the *Belgrano* went down, the conflict had been virtually bloodless—the only loss of life involved a small number of Argentinian commandos during the assaults on Port Stanley and South Georgia. The sinking of Argentina's cruiser was the real start of the fighting war, not the brief skirmishes a month before. It was, furthermore, illegal. After interviewing a member of the cabinet, Hugo Young concluded,

> The purpose of the war cabinet's apparently intense search for peace had been ... to make the British understand why they had to go to war; in other words, to maximize the chances that they would face and tolerate the casualties that were sure to come. From this it is hard

to avoid the conclusions that the peace efforts were in part a charade....[31]

Undoubtedly the Junta should have accepted the final UK peace proposal, even though it was drawn up to cast London in the best possible light and even though it was hard to swallow after the huge loss of life on the *Belgrano*.[32] But the British finely calculated that Galtieri was enough of a diplomatic pigmy to be out-manoeuvred, and he was. Nonetheless, Argentina only attacked because it did not believe that there would be a war. When the Thatcher government determined on a riposte, the Junta made concessions and offered to withdraw its forces. In response the British ordered the militarily needless and illegal—might we say aggressive?—sinking of the *Belgrano*, which ensured that a war did indeed take place. It was a crime even though the cruiser was a military target.

Since the end of the conflict in June various arguments in defence of the sinking of the *Belgrano* have been proposed. One is that it had Exocet missiles on board. But the cruiser and its escorts were hours away from the British task force and were not apparently heading towards it. Another claim is that after the *Belgrano* was sunk, the Argentinian navy was intimidated into staying in port, which was very helpful in the subsequent battle. This argument overlooks the obvious fact, however, that had the *Belgrano* not been destroyed there might not have been a full-scale military clash at all.

In her Cheltenham address, Thatcher claimed 'We fought to show that aggression does not pay and that the robber cannot be allowed to get away with his swag'. She likes a homely phrase and a simple moral to get the popular virtues of her politics across. To answer in kind—as far as her South Atlantic adventure is concerned—we may conclude by saying that two wrongs do not make a right.

At the End of the Day
On 20 May the House of Commons discussed the Falklands question on the eve of the landings. Thatcher opened the debate in trenchant style and concluded her speech with the following, which was presumably a carefully drafted final statement of her war aims, prior to the decisive fighting on the ground.

> The principles that we are defending are fundamental to everything that this Parliament and this country stand for. They are the principles of democracy and the rule of law. Argentina invaded the Falkland Islands in violation of the rights of peoples to determine by whom and in what way they are governed. Its aggression was committed against a people who are used to enjoying full human rights and freedom. It was executed by a Government with a notorious record in suspending and violating those same rights.

> Britain has a responsibility towards the Islanders to restore their democratic way of life. She has a duty to the whole world to show that aggression will not succeed and to uphold the cause of freedom.

We are now in a position to examine, clause by clause, this cardinal justification of the British military action.

(1) Britain must defend 'the principles of democracy and the rule of law'. The sinking of the *General Belgrano* was illegal and therefore criminal. It led to the collapse of the major peace talks. It was an action committed on the British side, almost certainly at Thatcher's orders. For democracy see below.

(2) 'Argentina invaded the Falkland Islands in violation of the rights of peoples to determine by whom and in what way they were governed.' It did so, but Argentina's claim to territorial sovereignty is good, while a people do not have an absolute right to determine that they should be ruled by a distant, expecially by a non-contiguous state. As we have seen from a glance at the Munich agreement of 1938, this fact—that the right of self-determination of peoples subject to overlapping territorial claims is *not* a decisive guide for policy—was established at a mighty cost in world war. While the rights of the Falklanders to the choice of their sovereignty was summarily 'violated', their right is not an absolute one (and none of them was killed).

(3) 'Argentina's aggression was committed against a people who are used to enjoying the full human rights and freedom.' This is a farcical description of the actual conditions in the British colony.

(4) 'It was executed by a Government with a notorious record in suspending and violating those same human rights.' Correct.

(5) 'Britain has a responsibility towards the Islanders to restore their democratic way of life.' In so far as they had such a life it was not immediately destroyed by Argentina's takeover. The dismissal of the Colonial executive was not a huge blow against local democracy. The local self-government of the islanders could and should have been improved and increased by the establishment of an autonomous, local administration, that could and should have been obtained under Argentina's sovereignty. That was the full extent of Britain's responsibility after the Junta's invasion—to ensure non-violently the preservation of local self-government.

(6) Britain 'has a duty to the whole world to show that aggression will not succeed and to uphold the cause of freedom'. The 'whole world' will come to its own conclusion about the British action and London's attitude towards aggression, one that is unlikely to accord with Thatcher's rhetoric about her desire for 'freedom'.

This leaves one last claim in Thatcher's statement of Britain's war aims in the Falklands: 'The principles that we are defending are fundamental to everything that this Parliament and this country stand for.' In so far as she describes the will and character of Parliament, we can do nothing but agree. But do the politics of Thatcher and Parliament represent what Britain stands for? Is *their* kind of sovereignty the one which its peoples will stand for now and forever? The answer will be contested.

8   The Logic of Sovereignty

THE SWIFT conclusion of the Falklands conflict has added to the unreality that surrounded the affair. The issue of the islands themselves will hardly disappear while the UK and Argentina remain in contention over them. But there is already a sense in which the intense battle of April to June 1982 seems to be receding into Britain's past. All the opposition parties, of course, have an obvious vested interest in shifting the media's attention from Thatcher's triumph. References to the Falklands Factor 'wearing off' can be heard with a stress that is clearly intended to hasten the process, as if the eruption of the war was merely an interference with the *real* politics of contemporary Britain. It is not hard to see why Michael Foot and his companions on the opposition front-bench (along with their Alliance counterparts) should feel this way. At the high point of his 'splendid' parliamentary challenge on 3 April, Foot must have felt that he would soon be walking through the door of No. 10, the new patriot summoned by the country in the moment of crisis. Instead, Thatcher drove home the sword he presented to her with his demand for 'deeds', and Foot's popularity rating slumped to a historic low.

By the same token, Thatcher's standing took on a new national dimension and she dominated the political stage by the war's end. The Conservatives began to harp on the enduring, long-term need for the 'spirit of the South Atlantic'. Nigel Lawson, one of the outstanding advocates of Thatcher's economic strategy, declared that 'the profound importance of this event cannot be overemphasized'. He was not referring to the EEC's decision to override British wishes on food prices, at once a major and humbling blow to the national 'sovereignty' and to the Government's anti-inflation drive. It was instead the South Atlantic that had captured Lawson's attention:

> The long years of retreat and self-doubt are over. A new self-respect, a new self-confidence, and a new sense of pride in ourselves has been born. It is the rebirth of Britain.[1]

The virtues of born-again nationalism will surely be sung to the next election if not beyond. In her Cheltenham attack on the train drivers' union and the hospital workers, Thatcher emphasized,

> We have to see that the spirit of the South Atlantic, the *real* spirit of Britain, is kindled not only by the war but can now be fired by peace.

Her partisan and class purpose are evident, but caution is needed before denying her claim. If the Falklands did not bring out *the* real spirit of Britain, the war certainly revealed *a* spirit of nationalism. Should we dismiss the Falklands adventure as an escapist interruption of what is actually British? Nigel Lawson's economic theories were in the process of erosion as they clashed with the stubborn noncompliance of British society. The true passion of the Falklands for him was almost certainly its contrasting decisiveness. Which was also what attracted Thatcher into battle in the first place. Just as it was the failure of Britain's industrial economy that propelled Thatcher into office, so the economic and political frustration she experienced, in turn, drove her to action rather than negotiation in the South Atlantic. The long relative economic decline and party political crisis of the UK determined the military diversion and remains its 'underlying' cause. That is why the war should not be seen as some kind of excrescence or interference in the normal run of things. If it was a minor 'accident', it was also part of the more general breakdown. Why bother with the 'form' of the crisis, when what we should be concerned about is its 'real' content? The short answer is simply, that content only appears in one form or another.

The longer answer concerns the need to project with plausibility a society different from Parliament's idea of Britain. For it must be emphasized again that while she exploited the opportunity it presented, the Falklands conflict was not just Thatcher's war. On the one hand, this means that her attempt to utilize the war for political purposes—to expropriate it as *her* demonstration of fortitude—may yet rebound to her discredit. On the other hand, it means that the left especially should not forget the powerful feelings of nostalgia and solidarity that the fighting engendered, sentiments that apparently engulfed a majority in all social classes.

The surprise was part of the trick in gaining their endorsement. For the dispatch of the fleet was not the result of any argued majority, let alone consensus, within the public domain. The crudity of the House of Commons had already done its work: before any discussion could begin the task force was a fact sailing over the horizon. Once force was deployed and secret 'negotiations' were underway, loyalty and trust was the first response. Once servicemen began to die, to say that they should not seemed to many at that moment like a gratuitous kick against those who had already paid the ultimate sacrifice. Their lives then remained as a testimony to the 'justice' of the cause, until victory itself smothered the sudden increase of British fatalities from 150 to 250 in its glorious winding sheet. Now that the war is over it remains difficult to point to the sheer *fatuousness* of spending upwards of £2,000 million to secure the Falklands, when successive governments have long said that they do not want the islands, and when £200 million would have brought the Kelpers much closer to a 'marvellous' and 'British' way of life, as Thatcher put it, than they have ever experienced or ever will. And that difficulty still comes from the deaths and the clash of sovereignty that have been involved.

So far as the dead are concerned, there stands the comment made by the mother of Mark Sambles, who was killed on HMS *Glamorgan*:

> I am proud of my son—but not proud of the fact that he died for his country in a war which was not necessary. I accept that it's a serviceman's duty to fight. But in a futile situation like this, I think it's evil to put men's lives at risk when negotiations around a table can save so much heartbreak.[2]

For Mrs Sambles it is 'evil' to put men's lives at risk when so much heartbreak could have been saved by negotiations around a table. Here—in contrast to its use by *The Times*—the word carries its full and proper meaning, stripped of incanted mysticism. And here too we can pause to consider the larger questions of sovereignty raised by any warlike engagement. For what is also remarkable about the comment of Mrs Sambles is that it could equally be applied to a larger international war of the great powers, if only because any nuclear exchange would also be futile, infinitely more so through its sheer destructive consequence.

We have seen in the Falklands an example of the logic of war. On the British side, the government was able not only to escalate but also deliberately and successfully, to induct the population into endorsing a mounting cost in ships and lives. Quite a lot has now been written about this in the greater scale, Edward Thompson especially has stressed the fearsome logic of nuclear weaponry. The Falklands War allows us to see rather clearly that there is another preliminary and constitutive force in addition to the intrinsic fatality of modern weapons, with their built-in timing and guidance systems. This is the 'logic' of national sovereignty itself.

Perhaps the best way to focus upon this is by reference to Jonathan Schell's recent book, *The Fate of the Earth*. He describes soberly and carefully, and thus with almost intolerable force, the way a nuclear exchange would probably destroy life on earth as the ecosphere was ripped apart. In his third and concluding section, he suggests that the only way to ensure that we can avoid this catastrophe is through the abandonment of the nation-state as the major organizing form of human society. From *Time* magazine downwards the grim exactitude of Schell's description of the fate which awaits us had been heralded. It is a 'must' for everyone to read. But his conclusions have been derided as somehow the unpractical musings of an author carried away by the pains of his imagination. How good of him to describe what might happen if the bombs went off; this is the fear the population has got to learn to live with. Yet how foolish of him to think that they could do without *us*, sovereign leaders—chosen of course—for their protection. Schell was not so naive as to fail to see that this would be the response:

> National sovereignty lies at the very core of the political issues that the peril of extinction forces upon us. Sovereignty is the 'reality' that the 'realists' counsel us to accept as inevitable, referring to any alternative as 'unrealistic' or 'utopian'.[3]

Is it in fact wrong to argue, as Schell does, that the choice is either 'utopia' or death?

Schell argues that 'nuclear powers put a higher value on national sovereignty than they do on human survival'. He also suggests that one of the factors that might drive the leaders of a nuclear power to retaliate against a first strike would be *revenge*. However futile and catastrophic the gesture, the desire for vengeance may override any 'statesmanlike' sobriety. Perhaps that 'gut instinct' is an essential attribute for 'statesmen', a measure of leadership quality. In March such an argument would have been dismissed as alarmist by commentators, who strive themselves for the judicious realism suitable to practical 'men of the world'. In Britain, in particular, such tones, at once patronising and dismissive run easily from the tongue. How could anyone suggest in this, the 'oldest' and 'most mature' democracy, where the accretions of the ages and the wisdom of experience may be found in the traditions of every establishment, that such a naked emotion as a mob desire for revenge might seize the *upper* classes?

Yet since Schell wrote, we have seen precisely a thuggish display of this sort. A second-rank but none the less nuclear power has sent its nuclear submarines and its ships almost certainly armed with tactical nuclear weapons into combat. (*Peace News* suggested that the *Sheffield* was sunk with nuclear depth charges on board.) What was the aim of this force? To wrest back sovereignty of an obscure and remote kind, and to salvage national pride, both of which were clearly ranked above the lives of the people directly concerned. Revenge was indeed the decisive passion.

Nor was this limited to mastodons from World War Two like 'Bomber' Harris. *Encounter* published two somewhat shamefaced reflections upon this emotion, neither by opponents of the war: one by Edward Pearce, the other by the magazine's columnist 'M'. This described how,

> I felt the bile rising like a gusher: stand back—I may explode. And what was I really angry about? The use of force, the violation of the peace, the subjugation of 1,800 Britons who don't want to be Argentines ... beneath the expressions of outrage were much more powerful, atavistic feelings. It was intolerable that Britain should be so humiliated ... Such was the immediate reaction—hardly less than .dancing in the streets of Buenos Aires ... Nor, of course, was I alone. Politicians of all classes were making similar noises.

'M' goes on to reflect upon this insane passion.

> What worried me about my own primitive feelings—to say nothing of other people's—was not only the danger of the Falkland Islands crisis, but the volatility of public opinion, likely to be just as fickle as fire.[4]

Now what is really interesting about this comment is that public opinion in Britain did *not* flare up with the same virulence. Perhaps twenty per cent of the population had a reaction like that of 'M', and doubtless the dinner parties he attended swilled with like sentiments. But it was not *public* demand for war that carried along reluctant and supposedly more far-sighted politicians. It was, on the contrary, the newspaper owners and MPs, the 'political' dons and military bureaucrats, who were most inflamed by the news. Why? Because for them *their* sovereignty, *their* world standing, *their* 'credibility' in the eyes of their equivalents abroad were at stake. This factor should not be underestimated as a pressure upon those for whom an international discourse is part of the daily routine of business. The idea that a Peruvian could smirk across the cocktails and make a joke about the 'Malvinas'; the idea that a German might sidle up and inquire what the British Navy was really *for*, after an arms expenditure since 1945 of £110 billion; the idea that a *Washington Post* staffer might commiserate with the *Telegraph* editorialist—these are the kind of things that constitute a 'national humiliation'. Our poor leaders experience such things personally.

At the beginning of this essay I considered at some length the conduct of Parliament on 3 April and glanced at every contribution made that day. What we saw was a record of collective irresponsibility. There was a general atmosphere of vindictiveness and revanchism in the Commons and those few who were prone to dissent were swiftly intimidated. Pearce vividly described it as a 'Hate-In'. The Prime Minister was egged on by her confidants, especially those whom she most trusted and who had been responsible for her promotion to the leadership of the Conservative Party. She did not conduct a 'madman' theory of war along the lines that Nixon had once hoped would frighten the Vietnamese into capitulation. Rather she personified the entire asylum of Britain's 'representatives'.

Which is why the Falklands affair stands as an exemplary vindication—if a minor one—of the general argument in *The Fate of the Earth*. Three aspects may be discerned. First, sovereignty is the special passion of those who deem themselves to be the leaders of a nation. For those 'at the top' and those who swarm around them, questions of sovereignty matter more extremely than for the majority of their compatriots. Those to whom our destiny is 'entrusted' project themselves as personages of experience and balanced judgement. In fact they may prove to be the most prone to react with speed and venom and a hysteria as fickle as fire. Second, when a nation's leaders have committed the state to 'do something', then the nation's 'credibility' is put on the line. 'Credibility' is something peculiarly attached to sovereignty, especially in any conflict: it suddenly becomes a factor which seems to be 'at risk' or about to be 'lost', especially in 'the eyes of others'. The word 'credibility' is American in its current geopolitical usage. In Britain the notion of 'standing' often takes its place. When people said that what was at stake in April was Britain's 'standing in the world', this was equivalent to Americans saying US 'credibility' was involved in Vietnam or Iran. Credibility becomes even more significant once weapons systems are openly put on alert or deployed. Once sabres are rattled a climb-down is all the more 'humiliating', and a greater blow to one's 'credibility'. But once men and weapons go into any engagement, then *their* military logic becomes a massive pressure for further action in its own way. There were some sobering examples of this during the Falklands War. The most striking—often repeated just before the landing at San Carlos—was that the task force could not be kept indefinitely in the winter seas of the South Atlantic: it had either to attack or return. The spokesmen who said this may have desired a landing, but that did not prevent what they said from being technically and hence 'neutrally' correct. So those in the peace movement who have emphasized the terrible casuistry of 'weapons-thought' and the logic of exterminism may be congratulated.

Finally what we can see more clearly thanks to the Falklands dispute is the dangerous *mix* of high technology and the 'sovereignty' of nation-states in decline. The system of the latter primes the former and puts it into play. Those who wear the mantle of greater patriotism and bear the responsibility of personifying a country's 'place in the world' may react almost instantaneously in a crisis, especially where their pride is at stake, where their opponents may strive to censure them and when they have been caught off guard. Their power and position then allows them to define the 'national

147

interest' before any public review, let alone democratic argument, has been heard. The logic of sovereignty is overswift and has no place for second thoughts. Meanwhile, the technological and military 'logic' of nuclear weapons systems places a greater and greater premium on the same immediate reactions of those who control their use.

We do not yet know, nor have seen created, those forms of direct, popular self-determination that could displace the curse of sovereignty. Any overall critique of the present lacks practical bite because of this absence. The Falklands crisis in Britain may demonstrate the need to present a socialist alternative to the politics of Britain's capitalist decline; if so, it also shows the need to transform the terms within which 'the nation' is itself conceived. The starting place for this is the House of Commons, because of the manifest decadence of its proceedings. Perhaps they make it too easy to mock. On the other hand they also reveal the complacency of the oft-heard defence of parliaments, that at least they are preferable to junta-like dictatorships. If that is their justification then such assemblies stand condemned: they are merely better than the worst. For whom is this good enough?

Meanwhile, the national institutions in London and Buenos Aires—Parliament and Junta alike—are also creations of the same international state system of competing sovereignties. Churchillism itself helped to form this embattled and demagogic global environment in 1945. Its imperial influence lives on. Thatcher justified the Falklands War by saying that the nation's honour was at stake. Many may snigger, but no major political challenge was mounted to combat, centrally and explicitly, the feeling she enunciated. This was the major defeat of the Falklands war. So long as the institutions and passions of nationalist sovereignty retain their domination, in Britain as elsewhere, the world will continue to be ruled by those who are likely to ensure its destruction.

Appendix

THE UNEXPURGATED THATCHER

Many of the quotations which have appeared in this essay may have seemed incredible or eccentric. Surely they do not represent the views of those in high office—the people in whose hands are placed our day-to-day destiny and the fateful power of nuclear weapons? Perhaps they have been cited out of context: one can only judge for oneself. Hence this appendix. Here one can read in full Margaret Thatcher's Cheltenham address, every word of it.

Conservative Central Office

NEWS SERVICE

Release time: 14.30 hours/SATURDAY, 3rd JULY, 1982
The Prime Minister
The Rt. Hon. Margaret Thatcher M.P.
(Barnet, Finchley)

SPEAKING TO A CONSERVATIVE RALLY AT CHELTENHAM RACE COURSE ON SATURDAY, 3rd JULY 1982

TODAY WE meet in the aftermath of the Falklands Battle. Our country has won a great victory and we are entitled to be proud. This nation had the resolution to do what it knew had to be done—to do what it knew was right.

We fought to show that aggression does not pay and that the robber cannot be allowed to get away with his swag. We fought with the support of so many throughout the world. The Security Council, the Commonwealth, the European Community, and the United States. Yet we also fought alone—for we fought for our own people and for our own sovereign territory.

Now that it is all over, things cannot be the same again for we have learned something about ourselves—a lesson which we desperately need to learn.

When we started out, there were the waverers and the fainthearts. The people who thought that Britain could no longer seize the initiative for herself.

The people who thought we could no longer do the great things which we once did. Those who believed that our decline was irreversible—that we could never again be what we were.

There were those who would not admit it—even perhaps some here today—people who would have strenuously denied the suggestion but—in their heart of hearts—they too had their secret fears that it was true: that Britain was no longer the nation that had built an Empire and ruled a quarter of the world.

Well they were wrong. The lesson of the Falklands is that Britain has not changed and that this nation still has those sterling qualities which shine through our history.

This generation can match their fathers and grandfathers in ability, in courage, and in resolution. We have not changed. When the demands of war and the dangers to our own people call us to arms—then we British are as we have always been—competent, courageous and resolute.

When called to arms—ah, that's the problem.

It took the battle in the South Atlantic for the shipyards to adapt ships way ahead of time; for dockyards to refit merchantmen and cruise liners, to fix helicopter platforms, to convert hospital ships—all faster than was thought possible; it took the demands of war for every stop to be pulled out and every man and woman to do their best.

British people had to be threatened by foreign soldiers and British territory invaded and then—why then—the response was incomparable. Yet why does it need a war to bring out our qualities and reassert our pride? Why do we have to be invaded before we throw aside our selfish aims and begin to work together as only we can work and achieve as only we can achieve?

That really is the challenge we as a nation face today. We have to see that the spirit of the South Atlantic—the real spirit of Britain—is kindled not only by war but can now be fired by peace.

We have the first pre-requisite. We know we can do it—we haven't lost the ability. That is the Falklands Factor. We have proved ourselves to ourselves. It is a lesson we must not now forget. Indeed it is a lesson which we must apply to peace just as we have learned it in war. The faltering and the self-doubt has given way to achievement and pride. We have the confidence and we must use it.

Just look at the Task Force as an object lesson. Every man had his own task to do and did it superbly. Officers and men, senior NCO and newest recruit—every one realized that his contribution was essential for the success of the whole. All were equally valuable—each was differently qualified.

By working together—each was able to do more than his best. As a team they raised the average to the level of the best and by each doing his utmost together they achieved the impossible. That's an accurate picture of Britain at war—not yet of Britain at peace. But the spirit has stirred and the nation has begun to assert itself. Things are not going to be the same again.

All over Britain, men and women are asking—why can't we achieve in peace what we can do so well in war?

And they have good reason to ask.

Look what British Aerospace workers did when their Nimrod aeroplane needed major modifications. They knew that only by mid-air refuelling could the Task Force be properly protected. They managed those complicated changes from drawing board to airworthy planes in sixteen days—one year faster than would normally have been the case.

Achievements like that, if made in peacetime, could establish us as aeroplane makers to the world.

That record performance was attained not only by superb teamwork, but by brilliant leadership in our factories at home which mirrored our forces overseas. It is one of the abiding elements of our success in the South Atlantic that our troops were superly led. No praise is too high for the quality and expertise of our commanders in the field.

Their example, too, must be taken to heart. Now is the time for management to lift its sights and to lead with the professionalism and effectiveness it knows is possible.

If the lessons of the South Atlantic are to be learned, then they have to be learned by us all. No one can afford to be left out. Success depends upon all of us—different in qualities, but equally valuable.

During this past week, I have read again a little known speech of Winston Churchill, made just after the last war. This is what he said:—

> We must find the means and the method of working together not only in times of war, and mortal anguish, but in times of peace, with all its bewilderments and clamour and clatter of tongues.

Thirty-six years on, perhaps we are beginning to re-learn the truth which Churchill so clearly taught us.

We saw the signs when, this week, the NUR came to understand that its strike on the railways and on the Underground just didn't fit—didn't match the spirit of these times. And yet on Tuesday, 8 men, the leaders of ASLEF, misunderstanding the new mood of the nation, set out to bring the railways to a halt.

Ignoring the example of the NUR, the travelling public whom

they are supposed to serve, and the jobs and future of their own members, this tiny group decided to use its undoubted power for what?—to delay Britain's recovery, which all our people long to see.

Yet we can remember that on Monday, nearly a quarter of the members of NUR turned up for work.

Today, we appeal to every train driver to put his family, his comrades, and his country first, by continuing to work tomorrow. That is the true solidarity which can save jobs and which stands in the proud tradition of British railwaymen.

But it is not just on the railways that we need to find the means and the method of working together. It is just as true in the NHS. All who work there are caring, in one way or another for the sick.

To meet their needs we have already offered to the ancillary workers almost exactly what we have given to our Armed Forces and to our teachers, and more than our Civil Servants have accepted. All of us know that there is a limit to what every employer can afford to pay out in wages. The increases proposed for nurses and ancillary workers in the Health Service are the maximum which the Government can afford to pay.

And we can't avoid one unchallengeable truth. The Government has no money of its own. All that it has it takes in taxes or borrows at interest. It's all of you—everyone here—that pays.

Of course, there is another way. Instead of taking money from our people openly, in taxation or loans, we can take it surreptitiously, by subterfuge. We can print money in order to pay out of higher inflation what we dare not tax and cannot borrow.

But that disreputable method is no longer open to us. Rightly this Government has adjured it. Increasingly this nation won't have it. Our people are now confident enough to face the facts of life. There is a new mood of realism in Britain.

That too is part of the Falklands Factor.

The battle of the South Atlantic was not won by ignoring the dangers or denying the risks.

It was achieved by men and women who had no illusions about the difficulties. They faced them squarely and were determined to overcome. That is increasingly the mood of Britain. And that's why the rail strike won't do.

We are no longer prepared to jeopardize our future just to defend manning practices agreed in 1919 when steam engines plied the tracks of the Grand Central Railway and the motor car had not yet taken over from the horse.

What has indeed happened is that now once again Britain is not prepared to be pushed around.

We have ceased to be a nation in retreat.

We have instead a new-found confidence—born in the economic

battles at home and tested and found true 8,000 miles away.

That confidence comes from the re-discovery of ourselves, and grows with the recovery of our self-respect.

And so today, we can rejoice at our success in the Falklands and take pride in the achievement of the men and women of our Task Force.

But we do so, not as at some last flickering of a flame which must soon be dead. No—we rejoice that Britain has re-kindled that spirit which has fired her for generations past and which today has begun to burn as brightly as before.

Britain found herself again in the South Atlantic and will not look back from the victory she as won.

Notes

1: Glare of War   pp. 15-23

[1] *Guardian*, 10 July 1982.
[2] *Economist*, 3 July 1982, p. 29; *Observer*, 11 July 1982.
[3] *Guardian*, 6 July 1982.
[4] *The Times*, 5 April 1982.
[5] Michael Foot, *Debts of Honour*, London 1980, p.55.
[6] After the debate on 20 May 1982, on the eve of the landings, 33 MPs voted against the use of force. Among them was Tony Benn (whose Falkland speeches can be read in *E.N.D. Papers 3*, Summer 1982); Tam Dalyell, the Labour spokesman for science, who fought Thatcher's militarism throughout; Andrew Faulds, Labour spokesman for the arts, who made a speech of outstanding vigour; Judith Hart, the current Chairperson of the Labour Party. Science and Art were promptly sacked as front-bench spokesmen, and were joined by Agriculture as Gavin Strang, Labour's spokesman for that industry, resigned, because although obliged to be absent from the vote he opposed the war. Two Plaid Cymru MPs also voted against the assault; their party was the only one to oppose the fighting officially.
[7] *London Review of Books*, 20 May 1982.
[8] At an oecumenical 'Teach-In Against the War', organized by the Socialist Society in London, 3 June 1982.

2: The Crackpot Parliament   pp. 24-45

[1] *Sunday Times*, 'Insight', 20 June 1982, based on research by Peter Beck.
[2] *Economist*, 19 June 1982.
[3] Martin Walker, *Guardian*, 19 June 1982.
[4] *Economist*, as cited. (My emphasis).
[5] *Ibid*.
[6] *Ibid*.
[7] *The Times*, 5 April 1982.
[8] John Shirley, *Sunday Times*, 20 June 1982.
[9] Interview on the 10.00 pm BBC News, 23 June 1982.
[10] 15 July 1982, p.21.
[11] Patrick Bishop, *Observer*, 20 June 1982.
[12] 'The 1980 census showed a population of 1,813 of which 1,360 were born in the Islands and 302 in Britain'. (*The Falkland Islands and Dependencies*, Reference Services, Central Office of Information, London March 1982. p.1.)

[13] All quotations from the debate are taken from *Hansard*.

[14] Foot's attitude is also a variant of what F.S. Northedge has termed the 'national arrogance', which he describes as 'the most persistent assumption in British thinking on foreign policy'. Namely: 'the idea that the rest of the world is rather like an unruly child which has a divine obligation to defer to its elders and betters like the British ... but which from time to time may be prevented from doing so by either sheer stupidity, or suppression by some upstart dictator ....' (*Descent from Power*, London 1974, p. 360).

[15] *Tribune*, 14 and 21 May 1982.

[16] Article 51 of the UN Charter reads: 'Nothing in the present Charter shall impair the inherent right of individual or collective self-defence if an armed attack occurs against a Member of the United Nations, until the Security Council has taken measures to maintain international peace and security'.

[17] In its lead editorial, 19 June 1982.

[18] *London Review of Books*, 20 May 1982.

3: Churchillism   pp. 46-62

[1] Keith Middlemas, *Politics in Industrial Society*, London 1979, p. 376.

[2] Later it included Communists although on a temporary basis, and also the 'British Road to Socialism', received its local inspiration from Churchillism, while the CPGB kept the 'Great' in its formal party name.

[3] Paul Addison, *The Road to 1945*, London 1977, p. 100.

[4] As above, p. 62. Addison's judgement in full is that the National Coalition resulted from 'the public shipwreck of a Conservative administration, and the corollary was that Labour were not in reality *given* office: they broke in and took it, on terms of moral equality'.

[5] This mimicked Leo Amery's famous parliamentary intervention on 2 September 1939, literally the eve of World War II, when he shouted across to the acting Labour leader Arthur Greenwood after Chamberlain had failed to announce an ultimatum for war: 'Speak for England, Arthur!'. A.J.P. Taylor, *English History, 1914-1945*, Oxford 1965, p. 452.

[6] Harold Wilson's father was a deputy election agent for Winston Churchill in 1908 when Churchill was standing as a liberal. Patricia Murray, *Margaret Thatcher*, London 1980, p. 94.

[7] Robert Dallek, *Franklin D. Roosevelt and American Foreign Policy, 1932-45*, New York 1979, p. 163.

[8] In 1938, 40% of all Latin American imports came from Britain, by 1948 only 8%, Gabriel Kolko, *The Politics of War*, London 1969, p. 493. Kolko is very clear on Anglo-American rivalry.

[9] Winston Churchill, *The Second World War*, vol. 3, London 1950, Chapter 24. For a discussion of the arguments this caused within British imperialist circles, see Wm. Roger Lewis, *Imperialism at Bay 1941-1945*, Oxford 1977, Chapter 6. Clause 5 of the Atlantic Charter provides an important addition for any discussion of Churchillism. While Roosevelt and Churchill were locked in their political struggle, the British War Cabinet back in London,

under Attlee's chairmanship and at Bevin's suggestion, proposed a further clause to the draft they were sent. This would proclaim improved labour standards, economic advancement and social security for all people. The supreme leaders agreed, but significantly rejected the suggestion that the 'abolition of unemployment and want' become a general war aim. Alan Bullock, *The Life and Times of Ernest Bevin*, vol 2, London 1967, p. 69. Bullock adds, 'It is impossible to read the Atlantic Charter now without a sense of disillusion, but at the time it raised great hopes. To Bevin it was a cause of some satisfaction that he had succeeded in getting both the British and American Governments to accept in principle the concern with the economic and social problems which he believed ought to figure as prominently as political factors in the post-war settlement.'

[10] But as Angus Calder points out, 'When Britain "stood alone", she stood on the shoulders of several hundred million Asians'. *Peoples War*, London 1971, p. 22.

[11] Middlemas, p. 272. His thoughtful study is welcome for its serious theoretical approach and sustained mastery of the primary sources—a rare combination. Its limitation, perhaps, is that Middlemas does not concern himself with the independent role of the City and overseas interests in the extended crisis of the British polity. See also, Leo Panitch, 'Trade Unions and the Capitalist State', NLR 125, January 1981, p. 27.

[12] Calder. p. 609.

[13] Churchill, vol. 4, p. 541.

[14] Bullock, p. 226.

[15] Calder, pp. 613-14.

[16] Martin Pugh, *The Making of Modern British Politics, 1867-1939*, Oxford 1982, p. 296.

[17] Tom Nairn. 'The Crisis of the British State'. NLR 132, November 1981. p. 40.

[18] Addison, p. 116.

[19] Henry Pelling, *Britain and the Second World War*, London 1970. p. 288.

[20] Andrew Gamble, *Britain in Decline*, London 1981, pp. 24-26.

4: Thatcherism   pp. 63-86

[1] For a good condemnation of this see Ralph Miliband's postscript in *Parliamentary Socialism*, second edn, London 1972, pp. 361-4.

[2] See my article, 'Heath, the Unions and the State', *NLR*, 77, January 1973.

[3] Martin Wiener, *English Culture and the Decline of the Industrial Spirit, 1850-1980*, Cambridge 1981, p. 163.

[4] T.F. Lindsay and Michael Harrington, *The Conservative Party, 1918-1979*, second edn, London 1979, p. 278.

[5] Margaret Thatcher, 'Let Our Children Grow Tall', speech of 15 September 1975, in *Selected Speeches, 1975-1977*, London 1977, p. 9.

[6] Ajit Singh, ' "Full Employment Capitalism" and the Labour Party', *The Socialist Register*, 1981, p. 12; a vivid summary of Thatcher's havoc.

[7] *Hansard*, 20 May 1981, p. 470.

[8] *Observer*, 25 February 1979, as cited by Hugh Stephenson, *Mrs Thatcher's*

First Year, London 1980.

[9] Winston Churchill, *The Second World War*, vol. 3, London 1950, p. 597.

[10] Keith Middlemas, *Politics in Industrial Society*, London 1979, p. 400.

[11] Anthony Sampson, *The Changing Anatomy of Britain*, London 1982, p. 46.

[12] Andrew Gamble, 'Mrs Thatcher's Bunker: the Reshuffle and its Consequences', *Marxism Today*, November 1981, p. 10.

[13] Malcolm Rutherford, 16 June 1982.

[14] Julian Critchley, 21 June 1982.

[15] Perry Anderson, 'Origins of the Present Crisis', *NLR* 23, January 1964. For E.P. Thompson's disagreement, see 'The Peculiarities of the English', in *The Poverty of Theory*, London 1978.

[16] *New Statesman*, 18 April 1975.

[17] See Tom Nairn's postscript to the new edition of *The Breakup of Britain*. Verso, London 1981, pp. 381-387.

[18] 'The Falklands Crisis'. *Encounter*, June-July 1982.

[19] *Economist*, 19 June 1982, p. 42. Parliament also gave him a mauling; for an important account of the Falklands debate of 4 December 1980, see Michael Davie, *Observer*, 30 May 1982.

[20] *Standard*, 23 June 1982, an embarrassing revelation.

[21] 11 June 1982.

[22] Peter Kellner wrote a devastating column on British secrecy and the constitutional, or rather the non-constitutional issues posed, *New Statesman*, 9 July 1982.

[23] *Guardian*, 9 June 1982.

[24] Especially as Raymond Whitney posed exactly this problem in the 3 April debate.

[25] Quoted in Miliband, p. 303.

[26] For example, Tom Nairn. *The Left Against Europe?* NLR 75, Sept. 1972.

[27] Stuart Hall, 'The Great Moving Right Show', *Marxism Today*, January 1979, a text of enviable foresight and judgement, written before Thatcher's election victory.

[28] *International*, May-June 1982: this is a variant of Gamble's explanation No. 1, while Thatcher's own view is No. 3.

[29] Of the nine, four made speeches in the 3 April debate (Sir Nigel Fisher, Russell Johnston, Ted Rowlands and Donald Stewart) and two others recorded questions or interruptions. For the full list, *Financial Times* 19 April 1982.

[30] *Hansard* for 20 May 1982, p. 519. Atkinson ended with the observation, 'He who dares, wins', the motto of the SAS.

[31] See Paul Kennedy's very useful survey, *The Realities Behind Diplomacy*, London 1981, p. 382.

[32] Correlli Barnett's *The Collapse of British Power*, London 1972, although pessimistic, suffers from this fault: the decline which it graphically describes is blamed upon the symptoms, when the cause was a world process that no amount of British power could have reversed.

[33] *The Times*, 17 November 1964.

[34] Quoted by Tom Nairn, 'British Nationalism and the EEC', *NLR* 69, September 1971, p. 4.

5: Pastoralism and Expatriotism   pp. 87-109

* I would like to thank Jane Kenrick for a helpful discussion about the themes of this chapter.

[1] *Economist*, 22 June 1892, which reported that 22% of its poll sample was against the victorious war 'given the cost in lives and money'.

[2] But the literary world did: one lead was given by James Fenton's passionate intervention in the *Spectator* 1 May 1982, which described the UK's Falklands adventures as 'frivolous, murderous and wicked'. A letter which denounced the war was signed by some of Britain's best novelists, from Angela Carter to Salmon Rushdie and was sent to *The Times*, which refused to publish it. For a more general picture see *Authors Take Sides on the Falklands*, London 1982, with its revealing pro-Armada statements from Spike Milligan to Arnold Wesker.

[3] *Guardian*, 14 August 1982.

[4] Tony Benn, *Parliament and Power*, London 1982, pp. 110-113.

[5] 16 June 1982.

[6] 16 June 1982.

[7] *Rule Britannia*, London 1981, pp. 184-8.

[8] August issue, 1982.

[9] 26 July 1982 (her emphasis).

[10] In a letter *The Times* did publish, 28 Mary 1982.

[11] See Walter Easey's Agenda article, *Guardian*, 26 April 1982.

[12] 31 May 1982.

[13] An off-the-cuff remark by Fred Halliday.

[14] David White, quoted by Martin Wiener, *English Culture and the Decline of the Industrial Spirit, 1850-1980*, Cambridge 1981, p. 78.

[15] pp. 48-9.

[16] *The Great War and Modern Memory*, Oxford 1979, pp. 231-5.

[17] As above, pp. 239-43. Fussell quotes R.H. Tawney, who said that during the Somme attack, one of his men 'Buried his head to the ground and didn't move. I think he was crying. I told him I would shoot him, and he came up like a lamb'. Mutinous French troops would make a loud *baa*-ing noise as they were being marched to the front line.

[18] As above, p. 51 ff.

[19] *Hansard* for House of Lords, 3 April 1982, p. 1583.

[20] Wiener, p. 158.

[21] *The Country and the City*, London 1975, p. 356. Fraser Harrison's important essay *Strange Land; the countryside myth and reality*, London 1982, draws upon Williams' work amongst others to make a novel plea for rural values that is also a critique of nostalgic pastoralism.

[22] 10 pm BBC radio news, 17 June 1982.

[23] 'Working class culture and politics in London, 1870-1900: notes on the remaking of a working class', *Journal of Social History*, Summer 1974.

[24] *Observer*, 31 July 1982.

[25] *Standard*, 15 June 1982.

[26] 3 July 1982.

[27] As above.

[28] As above.

[29] *Financial Times*, 20 July 1982.

[30] Letter to *The Times*, 17 June 1982.

[31] *Guardian* Parliamentary report for 10 June 1982.

[32] Winston Churchill, *The Second World War*, vol II, London 1949, p. 307.

[33] Phillip Knightley, *The First Casualty*, London 1982, p. 84.

[34] A.J.P. Taylor, *English History, 1914-1945*, Oxford 1965, pp. 60-1.

6: A War in the Third World   pp. 110-117

[1] The schema is sufficiently broad to absorb the fact that Somalia has seen much less terror than Ethiopia, for the main point is that the latter country has undergone a more profound social transformation.

[2] *New York Times*, 2 May 1982; *Guardian*, 1 June 1982.

[3] On the important questions of arms sales and the Falklands, see Mary Kaldor, *Guardian*, 17 May 1982. Ian Watson, Deputy City Editor of the *Sunday Telegraph*, noted cheerfully, 'Nobody may like to see headlines like "Galtieri is good for GEC", or "It's take-off time for defence shares", but that's the world we live in.' To which the appropriate response is surely, 'For how long?'; *The Magazine*, June 1982.

[4] Not to mention all the Third World conflicts of the recent past—the wars of the Indian sub-continent, the fighting around the periphery of China, the Israeli wars in the Middle East....

7: A Just Settlement?   pp. 118-141

[1] See Nigel Williamson, *Tribune*, 25 June 1982, for a useful summary of this episode. Also, John Madely, 'Diego Garcia: a contrast to the Falklands', *Minority Rights Group*, Report 54 (36 Craven St., London WC2; £1.20).

[2] See A.J.P. Taylor, *English History, 1918-1945*, Oxford 1965, p. 426, who notes that the *New Statesman* took a similar stand.

[3] Keith Middlemas, *Diplomacy of Illusion*, London 1972, pp. 346 and 375.

[4] London, 1982, pp. 51 and 53.

[5] Middlemas, as cited, p. 341.

[6] 15 April 1982.

[7] Lord Shackleton and others, *Economic Survey of the Falkland Islands*, London 1976.

[8] *Guardian*, 30 April 1982.

[9] *The Times*, 29 April 1982.

[10] Latin American Bureau, *The Falklands—Malvinas, Whose Crisis?* (forthcoming).

[11] *The Times*, 3 June 1982.

[12] Patrick Bishop, *Observer*, 20 June, 1982.

[13] Gareth Parry, *Guardian*, 3 July 1982.

[14] John Witherow, *The Times*, 29 June 1982.

[15] 9 August 1982.

[16] *Sunday Times*, 1 August 1982. Winchester's report was especially notable for its lack of sentimentality as he was jailed in Argentina for most of the war.

[17] Robin Fox, *Listener*, 15 July 1982.

[18] *Listener*, 8 July 1982. Could it have been that the '2 Para' knew, as Fox did not, that they were if anything the Persians at Thermopylae....

[19] Anthony Arblaster, *The Falklands. Thatcher's War, Labour's Guilt*, a spirited Socialist Society pamphlet (available from 7 Carlisle Street, London W.1., £1).

[20] The list is taken from a *Sunday Times'* sketch of the War Cabinet, 30 May 1982. In addition, Clive Whitmore, Thatcher's principal private secretary, attended most War Cabinet Meetings; see *Guardian*, 23 July 1982.

[21] *Sunday Telegraph*, 4 July 1982.

[22] *The Times*, 7 May 1982.

[23] Speech to the Welsh Conservative Conference, *Guardian*, 14 June 1982.

[24] *Guardian*, 12 June 1982, in the Terry Coleman interview.

[25] *Sunday Times*, 13 June 1982

[26] John Walcott, *Newsweek*, 24 May 1982.

[27] Hugh Trevor-Roper, *Daily Telegraph*, 28 May 1982.

[28] *The Times*, 29 April 1982, reproduced in *Zero Option*, London 1982.

[29] John Shirley, *Sunday Times*, 20 June 1982.

[30] Interview with President of Peru, Fernando Belaúnde Terry, *Newsweek*, 7 June 1982.

[31] *Sunday Times*, 4 July 1982.

[32] For the full text of the 'final' British position, *The Times*, 21 May 1982.

8: The Logic of Sovereignty   pp. 142-148

[1] *Financial Times*, 29 June 1982.

[2] *Bridport News*, 18 June 1982, quoted in *Tribune*, 25 June 1982.

[3] Jonathan Schell, *The Fate of the Earth*, London 1982, p. 218.

[4] *Encounter*, June-July 1982, p. 33.